UNCOOKED

LYNDSAY AND PATRICK MIKANOWSKI

PHOTOGRAPHS BY GRANT SYMON

UNCOOKED

Flammarion

Contents

32 | 34 ingredients and more than 100 recipes

Preface

Why write a cookbook about foods that are all served uncooked? The answer is quite simple. Eating raw food—whether fish or meat, vegetables or fruit, dairy products, herbs, or spices—is good for you; these foods are delicious and easy to prepare. The finished dish will provide lots of vitamins and trace elements in return for fewer calories; quite a bonus for the majority of us who lead sedentary lives. Raw fruit and vegetables are beneficial for health as they contain not only nutritional elements but also the fibers that are indispensable for internal balance. The USDA recommends eating at least one raw fruit and one raw vegetable per day. By varying your raw fruit and vegetables, you will master the art of how to use them to their best advantage, and learn how to love them more.

Meat and fish should not be ignored either, because they can be delicious if eaten uncooked. You will find yourself consuming smaller portions, because you will feel satisfied more quickly if you have eaten them raw. Meat and fish contain

Fall harvest.

proteins that are coverted into amino acids during digestion. Once the liver's immediate metabolic needs are satisfied, it converts superfluous protein molecules into glucides and fatty acids. These are stored in the body as (often excess) weight. By cutting down on the amount of protein you eat, you will be reducing the opportunity for your liver to have to do this kind of conversion, so you'll be putting on fewer pounds.

There is another good reason why it is advisable to cut down on the amount of animal protein you consume. Livestock rearing is very costly in environmental terms and, when pushed to the extremes of viability, can even become a public health risk. If people ate more plant protein, these risks would be lessened. Meat that is sold very cheaply is often produced from animals fed on nutritional and energy supplements; these are designed to make an animal grow fast—too fast. At best, these animals are given plant fodder that relies for its production on the expenditure of large amounts of water and chemical fertilizers; at worst, these animals may be fed on supplements of more dubious origins. Some may contain molecules created using the latest chemical techniques (of which the legislators may still be largely unaware), or meal and flours—e.g. bone meal and other products of animal origin—such as those that led to bovine spongiform encephalopathy (BSE or "mad cow disease"). The lesson must be that it is better to choose a quality meat sold at a correspondingly high price, purchased rarely and served sparingly.

There are numerous "raw" dairy products on the market that are made from pasteurized milk, such as yogurt, cream, and goat's- or ewe's-milk cheese, in addition to the soft cheeses such as Camembert, which can be chosen according to the season. Remember that all these products, and especially fruit and vegetables, offer better value for money if bought in season; if you buy locally you will also avoid the added costs and pollution that transportation necessarily involves.

This book lists a range of uncooked foods that will enable you to create dishes using raw foods that are in season, and to understand how to use uncooked foods in various ways.

So why not eat uncooked? And does that mean you can only eat uncooked foods? Not at all! That sort of fundamental approach can only lead to disappointment. Never tasting freshly baked bread again, abandoning spaghetti carbonara, or saying goodbye for ever to chili con carne would be to adopt a food monoculture that might even be harmful in the long term. Furthermore, bringing along your own bag of raw food when you're invited to dinner might result in interesting table talk at first, but your friends—and you—would soon grow tired of it, and it's not exactly flattering to the hosts. Variety, the key to success, applies just as much to what you eat as to anything else. It is by varying your daily diet that you will keep in shape, benefiting your health as well as your social life.

Why eat

uncooked foods?

Why eat uncooked foods?

Let us take a closer look at uncooked foods. The flavors and textures, the shapes and colors of raw foods are unfamiliar. In order to eat raw meat, fish, and vegetables, you will need to learn new ways of cutting, slicing, crushing, shredding, and marinating, so as to develop the true flavor of the foods and help you digest them. It is a good opportunity to learn how to use kitchen appliances that slice, emulsify, and blend. There are also hand-operated utensils that make it easier to work with raw ingredients, such as the grater, the mandoline, and the vegetable mill. Their abrasive action breaks down the cell walls of foods by fragmenting them, thus increasing the surface exposed to the digestive juices, and making digestion more efficient.

By gradually getting used to the taste of raw foods, new gastronomic pleasures will be discovered, through the creation of original combinations of meat and vegetables, fish and fruit, or crustaceans and herbs. You will need to learn to mix textures—crunchy with creamy, for example. This is a difficult combination to obtain using cooked ingredients, but easy with food items served raw. Jellies, sauces, and marinades add a further flexibility to uncooked foods, as well as looking appetizing and

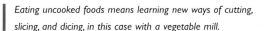
Eating uncooked foods means learning new ways of cutting, slicing, and dicing, in this case with a vegetable mill.

attractive. You will also need to learn how to chop, thinly slice, carve, roll up, and shape the raw ingredients.

Color is of particular importance when serving raw foods. You can create single-color presentations or use contrasting colors, without having to worry about what color changes might occur during the cooking process. Cooking tends to dull the color of food; by preparing uncooked dishes, you will find yourself presenting foods in glorious full color.

All of the skill and pleasure of this type of cuisine lies in arranging the food on the plates; that is to say, in assembling what has been prepared on individual dishes for each diner before serving. This is essential to ensure that uncooked foods are presented to their best advantage.

Allow plenty of time for arranging the food on the plate, time that would otherwise be spent in cooking the food. You will quickly begin to enjoy the art of combining and contrasting complementary flavors, colors, shapes, and textures. When you go shopping for food, first

Scallops and passion fruit, an unusual combination that is rich in color, flavor, and has an unusual shape (see recipe page 104).

make a list of all the ingredients, noting down the colors, shapes (roughly), and the textures you are looking for. Within these broad guidelines, you can then make your decisions on final purchases based on what is available in the stores— on what is in season, or on the freshness of the product. It is also very helpful to accept recommendations from your suppliers: they will be able to point you to the best and freshest produce on offer.

Accept only the best

You will soon learn to improvise, based on ideas that will come to you while you are making your purchases. It is only by appreciating the quality of the produce when seeing it for yourself that you can choose the best ingredients. That is why the choice of raw food should be based on the best produce available in the market, using only the most reliable suppliers.

Today, we are spoiled for choice in terms of the range of foods that can be served uncooked. Consequently, in order to narrow down your options in terms of

purchases, you need to take a variety of criteria into consideration: among those are flavor, freshness, seasonality, provenance, and the way in which the food was grown or raised. Again, it is always a good idea to get advice from the experts.

However, there are two main aspects of quality that will guarantee the success of uncooked food. These are absolutely essential in all circumstances—flavor and freshness. We know that freshness of ingredients is always important for a cooked dish; it becomes essential where the foods are served raw. Assessing the quality of the foods is also a matter of individual know-how—one's own and that of one's suppliers. Always keep your nose and taste buds on the alert, and always ask to taste the food first, if at all possible. There is a Japanese word that is used to describe the essence of an excellent food: "*umami,*" whose literal meaning is "the quality of that which is delicious." The equivalent in the West is the ability to recognize a good piece of meat, knowing what a fish looks like when it has just come out of the water, memorizing the flavor of the first garden peas of the season—when they have not yet become floury and dry but are still sweet and juicy. Insist on fragrant, juicy oranges and heavily scented herbs. Over time, you will acquire an education in the art, but you will need to study this art just like all others—by reading, thinking, and through practical work.

In terms of freshness, whether the food is produced locally or far away is no longer particularly relevant. This is thanks to modern preservation methods, which keep the produce constantly chilled or frozen (the cold chain), and to the speed of transport these days in international trade. So, whether a food tastes good or not does not depend so much on the number of miles it has had to travel from its place of production to the plate. The best way of learning how to buy food at its best is to pay special attention to your suppliers, choosing the best you can find. Be demanding. But be aware that excellence has its price, usually a high one, and this does not necessarily include the cost to the environment nor the social cost. Excellence should not be acquired to the detriment of someone else's well-being. Responsible behavior—protecting individuals and the environment—means questioning and being informed in order to understand fully the conditions in which the foods you buy were produced.

Memorize the flavor and texture of the first garden peas of the season.

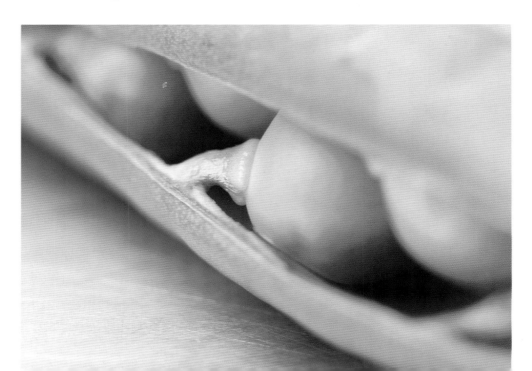

Why eat uncooked foods?

Curiosity and traceability

Your suppliers are people to whom you should devote special attention. Your fishmonger, butcher, and green grocer are all people that you go to regularly because you have conducted a thorough investigation and regard them as the most reliable sources of your food. Consult the trade and specialists, get recommendations from gourmet friends, cooks, and from any chefs you know, and do a lot of testing yourself.

Suppliers who care—who are really engaged in their work—will facilitate traceability.

However, once that rare pearl—a reliable supplier—has been found, have confidence in him or her. Always explain to your supplier what you intend to prepare in terms of uncooked food. The various ways of cutting and slicing meat and fish are important for enhancing both the look and taste of the food.

As for fresh vegetables, growing your own is a good way of acquiring additional knowledge, combining horticulture and gastronomy. You will learn which varieties you can grow easily and which taste the best; you will also find out which will add special notes of color or texture. A vegetable garden is an assurance that you will have access to produce of incomparable freshness and sublime flavor. However, as we have noted, there are also merchants at farmer's markets and other produce suppliers who will share your curiosity and themselves grow a range of superb vegetables.

The supply network that has been opened up through Internet mail order is an excellent new way of obtaining produce.

Joël Thiébault,
an inquisitive gourmet truck farmer.

It is by testing out all these alternatives that you will find suppliers who meet the criteria of providing freshness and flavor, and who will keep you informed about their own sources of supplies. Sellers who care—who are really engaged in their work—are your guarantee of traceability. This means being able to find out about production methods, "best before" dates, and the geographical origin of the food product.

Demand for the highest standards will also extend to international foods, since nowadays cuisine is increasingly drawing its inspiration from all over the world, breaking down the barriers of frontiers and seasons. It is easy these days to find tropical foods; they are indispensable for this type of uncooked cuisine and their quality is subject to stringent growing and transportation requirements.

Although the supermarket chilled and freezer sections are well stocked with fruit and vegetables, the flavor of the product is unlikely to be their prime concern. Avoid prepackaged foods if possible, because you won't be able to check them easily. Cellophane and polystyrene severely restrict your vision; you will not be able to smell the contents of the package either. Apart from anything else, too much packaging is damaging from an environmental point of view. Watch out for foods that are not at the peak of freshness. Look at the "best before" dates on the packaging. You may have to scour the shelves to find products whose "best before" date is the most recent—be aware that the oldest foods are usually stocked at the front, so the freshest produce will be at the back.

Then again, it's best to avoid fruit and vegetables that look immaculate. They have probably been purchased from growers who use large amounts of pesticides and fertilizers and practice artificial irrigation. Excessive use of pesticides harms the environment and also has public health implications. Too much watering reduces flavor and too much fertilizer makes plants less resistant to predators (meaning more pesticide has to be applied to the plants, and so the process goes on).

Supermarket meat and fish also tend to suffer from a surfeit of packaging. As with the fruit and vegetables, it is hard to inspect them properly; with all the pretrimming and prepackaging it is also not as easy to find the cut of meat or fish that you want. And who do you complain to if something isn't right with your purchases? Do all supermarkets care as much about their suppliers as you do? The pursuit of profit is clearly the prime consideration of all mass-production operations, and this does not necessarily result in quality produce. This can also hurt the smaller farmers who do not have the means to stand up effectively to the supermarkets. The results are often self-evident.

Freshness and hygiene

There is another very good reason for eating uncooked foods today, and it is by no means the least important. The incredible progress made in the adoption of the cold chain method at all stages of agribusiness (production, transportation, marketing, and consumption) has resulted in an incomparable amount of choice, quality, and freshness of produce, and a massive expansion in terms of availability of foodstuffs. Food hygiene regulations are stringent, and many checks and inspections are performed by federal and state supervisory authorities. It is not in a

Zucchini fruit and blossoms.

company's interest to be caught breaking the rules. The consequences could badly affect its income.

The legislation concerning the safety of raw foods should serve as a reminder—not only of the importance of taking special precautions when you cook raw (what an oxymoron!), but also in terms of reinforcing habits that ought to be your general practice when you cook in your own home. Adherence to strict food hygiene practices is absolutely vital, even when cooking food, and when preparing to serve uncooked dishes these hygiene practices should be even more closely observed. A whole series of measures are presented here that will explain clearly how to buy, store, clean, and prepare uncooked foods. These measures will minimize the risks that can lie in wait when pathogens are not destroyed by heating, as happens when the foods are cooked.

In the best of shape

The association between food and hygiene encourages us to address also the link between food and a healthy lifestyle. In the context of this book, in which fruit and vegetables predominate, we feel that it is a good idea to promote healthy eating, especially given today's propensity for "fast-food nations."

When the World Health Organization (WHO) met in Geneva in May 2004, it stressed the importance of the role of fruit and vegetables in the diet. It recommends a daily intake of an average of 14 oz (400 g). There are other recommendations by the WHO, the United States Food and Drug Administration (FDA), and the U.S. Department of Agriculture (USDA). In combination with a balanced diet in which the consumption of animal proteins is restricted, adopting these recommendations can rapidly correct the effects of an unhealthy diet.

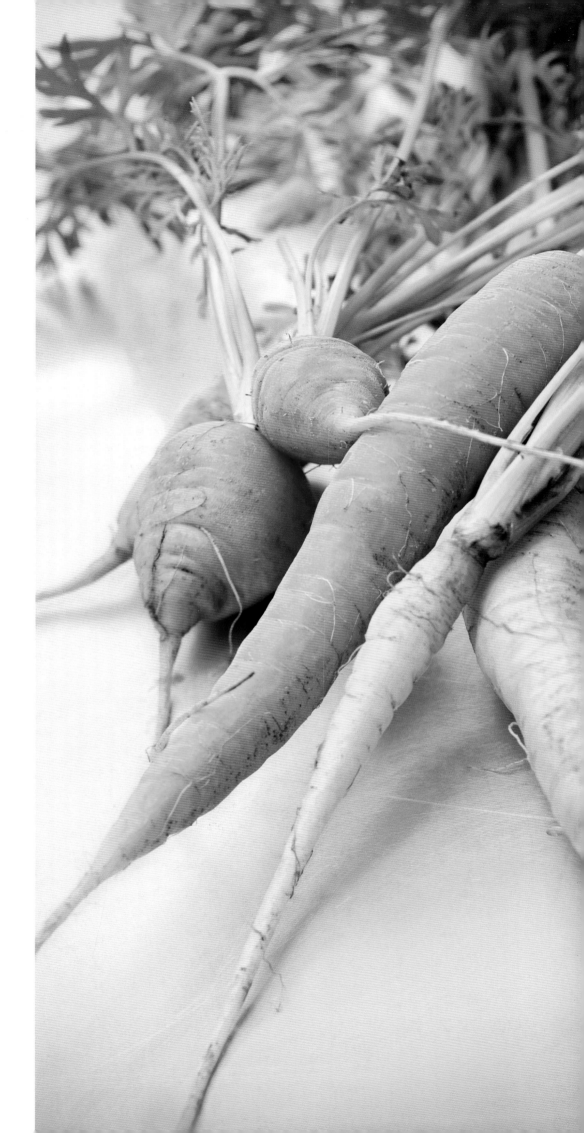

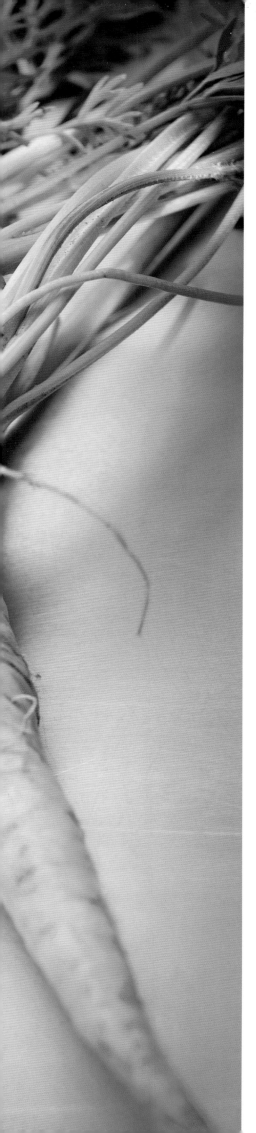

Why eat uncooked foods?

The world explosion in obesity and degenerative diseases, such as cardiovascular disease, cancer, and diabetes, is about to become a global health problem of mega proportions. Cardiovascular disease is the primary cause of death in industrialized countries, accounting for a third of the causes of mortality worldwide and, as with obesity, the situation is getting worse every year. Type 2 (late-onset) diabetes is very much on the increase. There are currently around 150 million people worldwide suffering from this condition, and the figure is due to double by 2005. These pathologies are the subject of expensive treatments that do not necessarily work. In France, for example, incidences of cancer, taking all types together, increased by 63 percent between 1980 and 2000. Tobacco and alcohol are no longer the only culprits; diet may also be a cause of cancer.

Being overweight is a risk to health because it can contribute to the development of cancer. The risk from cancer is minimal when the body mass index (BMI) is maintained at between 18.5 and 25. The BMI is calculated by dividing weight by height in inches squared and multiplying by 703. This means that according to international recommendations, an adult should not put on more than 9 lb (5 kg) in his/her entire adult life.

The upshot is that people need to eat less and maintain moderate physical activity (at least half an hour's walk a day, for example) and vigorous activity (at least two hours of intense fitness activity per week) throughout their lives. Drinking plenty of water and drinking wine in moderate quantities—that means two glasses per day at the most and never if you are going to drive—and cutting out tobacco completely can only extend your

life as a sporting gourmet, while very much improving your quality of life. Uncooked foods can make a contribution to this lifestyle because raw foods are nutritious but also low in calories. So eating uncooked is a way of reconciling the life of a gastronome with a cuisine—and by this I mean the transformation of ingredients without resorting to cooking them—that pampers you without spoiling your health.

Raw and cooked

In a book entitled *Le Cru et le Cuit (The Raw and the Cooked)*, first published in French in 1964, the anthropologist Claude Lévi-Strauss claimed that a structural analysis of myths and legends reveals, through a series of contrasts and contradictions (e.g. high/low, hot/cold, raw/cooked), a description of the conscious or unconscious rules of social organization. According to his analysis of mythology, the origins of an ordered society began with "the discovery of the cooking of foods," which is the "criterion for transition from nature to culture."[1] Thus, Lévi-Strauss maintains, uncooked is the opposite of cooked and has a

The World Health Organization recommends an average daily consumption of 14 oz (400 g) of fruit and vegetables.

Why eat uncooked foods?

A potato field in bloom.

connotation that associates it with nature, in the nature/culture dichotomy, i.e., cooked and socialized or uncooked and natural. By uniting opposites—the heavens (the gods) and earth (the human race) in the creation of myths; fire and water in cooking food; man and woman in marriage—societies construct categories that enable them to "think" about their relationship with the world around them. According to Lévi-Strauss, through their mythologies, societies formalize the condition essential for their survival—exchange. Exchange of goods, opening up to others, accepting "a social life that goes beyond the bounds of the group."[2] *Le Cru et le Cuit* is the first volume in a series of four books of which the last, entitled *L'Homme nu (The Naked Man)*, "comes back to the beginning, because in terms of culture, naked is the equivalent of raw in relation to nature."[3]

Cooked and raw

From the end of the Neolithic period (c. 3300 BCE), the populations of the great settled civilizations of the Old World and the New lived on a very monotonous diet for centuries. Their food, which only varied according to their geographical location, consisted almost exclusively of grains (rice in Asia; wheat, barley, and rye in Europe and the Middle East; maize in South America), supplemented by a few root vegetables (turnips and carrots), and sometimes legumes (such as beans in the Mediterranean basin) or tubers (potatoes among the Incas), accompanied by cabbage or onion in antiquity. To these might be added a very small amount of meat and fish for the privileged few on special occasions. Some vegetables were pickled in salt or vinegar, but you needed the means to buy these preserving agents.

The diet was thus based on foods of vegetable origin. Rice, wheat, corn, beans, and a few potatoes were grown for their high energy value and also because, if harvested ripe, they could be stored for long periods, thus making it possible to survive in bad times—drought or cold— without starving. These foods also performed a specialized role in social functions. The farmers provided sustenance for those who devoted their energies to politics or religion. One could actually, thanks to these very special foods, store and transfer wealth in the form of nourishment.

However, all of these foods required heat treatment in order for them to be usable by humans because they were high in starch (a high-energy substance) that requires cooking for it to be digested. So cooking has always dominated food preparation throughout human society.

A small supplement of fruit and plants, provided through gathering food in the wild or from gardening, offered an additional seasonal treat for those who harvested them. Fruit and a few herbaceous plants, such as lettuce, were eaten raw. These were important for their nutritional value in terms of vitamins and trace elements, but such foods remained marginal and were consumed only occasionally. Scurvy, an illness caused by a lack of vitamin C (a vitamin present in many raw fruit and vegetables), is characterized by a number of symptoms— fever, anemia, bleeding, gastroenteritis, and excessive weight loss leading to death. It was not only sailors on long voyages (lasting months or even years at a time) that suffered from scurvy; it once ravaged whole populations. Towns and villages all over Europe were affected by this almost endemic disease. Generally, fruit were stored and used as reserves. It was not until the Renaissance in Europe, when sugar became more widely available, that fruit could be made into jams and jellies. Before this, drying techniques were used. Some fruit, such as apples, apricots, figs, and grapes, would keep well after drying if the climate was suitable.

On the other hand, trade between different parts of the world, which had begun in antiquity (from the eighth century BCE), favored the circulation of food plants. Later, in the Middle Ages (fourth–fifteenth centuries), trade routes opened up throughout Europe and became worldwide, thanks to voyages to the Orient and the discovery of the New World, which the Portuguese and Spaniards accomplished in less than a century (1480–1564). The British, French, and Dutch took up the challenge during the next century. Europe became the hub for the transfer of edible plants between the East, Oceania, Africa, and the New World.

The eggplant originated in India but is now considered a classic ingredient of Mediterranean cuisine.

Lemons reached Europe from China in the Middle Ages.

The melon is a member of the squash family and comes from the Old World.

After the conquest of the mainland and the setting up of a port on the Pacific coast of the isthmus of Central America, the tomato was taken in a Spanish galleon from its ancient Aztec land to the Philippines. It was eventually planted throughout Asia. It reached Europe by the same means; as did the potato, cultivated by the Incas, which transformed the European diet in the nineteenth century. This diaspora of food plants expanded even farther during the twentieth century.

Once the cultivation of these plants had been mastered (many were frost-sensitive, for example, and so needed special care), these new fruit and vegetables were soon grown all over the world and on a local level. Large-scale production for an expanded market was only made possible by the European agricultural and industrial revolution of the eighteenth and nineteenth centuries, which supplied the means to cultivate, finance, and—above all—rapidly transport the resulting harvests. This made it possible to send fresh fruit and vegetables ever greater distances to new markets. Previously, certain produce such as tomatoes, eggplant, and chili peppers had to be dried after harvesting. They were regularly preserved in the countries around the Mediterranean and could thus be marketed more easily.

The train, the steamship, and now motorized transport such as the trucks that travel the long, safe, well-maintained highways, encourage international trade. Today, isothermal containers are loaded on cargo airplanes to bring tropical vegetables and fruit to the inhabitants of North America and northern Europe, imprisoned in their temperate climate.

The early twentieth century witnessed the cultivation and marketing, far from their original birthplace, of food plants of subtropical origin. Tomatoes from the Mediterranean, pineapples from Hawaii and Senegal, avocados from Mexico, and lemons, oranges, and other citrus fruit from North Africa or Florida—all sail the seven seas. At first, canning was used to preserve and transport the most delicate fruit such as tomatoes and pineapples. The shores of the Mediterranean still bear the trace of this major industry, as can be seen from the buildings—now put to other uses but still often flanked by a tall chimney—used for cooking the fruit. The word "tangerine" is derived

Merchants, conquistadors, Jesuits, seafarers, and adventurers brought food plants to the Americas. These foods included wheat, European vines, sugar cane (brought to Europe from India during the Middle Ages), and the olive tree. Fortunes made and missions accomplished, a few of them sailed home again, bringing back with them plants grown by farmers before the arrival of Christopher Columbus.

All these plants gradually changed and shaped the cuisines of the world. For instance, where would the curries of Asia be without the hot chili peppers originally grown by the pre-Columbian farmers? The eggplant, which comes from India, is now a key ingredient in Mediterranean cuisine. And try to imagine Mediterranean food without the tomato, or the zucchini (a member of the squash family), both of which hail from central America. Members of this same family from the Old World—such as the melon from Africa and the cucumber from northern India—have spread worldwide. The lemon and the orange, which reached Europe from China in the Middle Ages, became acclimatized in southern Europe; they then arrived in the West Indies with Christopher Columbus during his second voyage (1493–96).

Symbols of modern life: cucumbers all year round.

Why eat uncooked foods?

seasons because new horticultural techniques enabled these plants to grow outside their natural environment. The Dutch are a people who have been changing their environment for centuries, and were the first to start cultivating subtropical fruit and vegetables in glasshouses; the polder dams became the new tropics. Dutch cucumbers, bell peppers, tomatoes, eggplant, and strawberries are sold all over Europe and are found on market pushcarts throughout the year. In Southern Spain growers copied the success of the Netherlands, but the climate there meant they did not have to heat the glasshouses. Semitrailers from Spain travel all over Europe to deliver vegetables and fruit that were once considered rare and exotic but are now commonplace.

| The pear, a native of China.

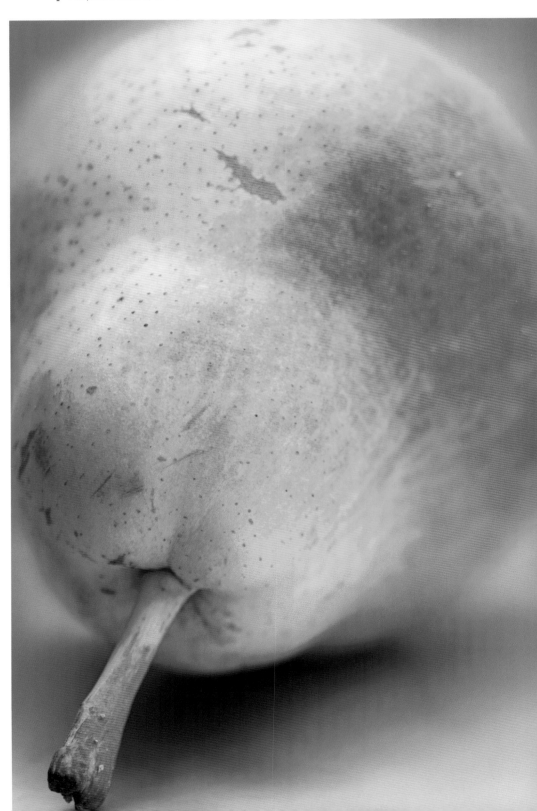

| Bell peppers grown under glass.

from the city of Tangiers, which for many years served as the port from which this fruit was exported from North Africa to Europe.

This massive expansion in the availability of fresh fruit and vegetables throughout all levels of the population has resulted in better knowledge of these foods. The consumption of raw fruit and vegetables started to become popular after World War II, amid the euphoria of a higher standard of living. First the North American, then the European consumer discovered modern life and the delights of new flavors in cooking. It became more and more easy to find bananas, avocados, citrus fruit such as grapefruit, and other tropical fruit that were eaten raw. Avocados, bananas, and citrus fruit survive journeys well because they can be picked while still green and will continue to ripen. This means they can be harvested and sold before they are fully ripe.

Once the fruit and vegetables had crossed borders, they could forget about climates and overcome the problem of

These racks are ideal for ripening tomatoes in summer or for storing potatoes in a root cellar.

With the rise of international transportation, one problem still remained to be solved. How could fragile tropical produce be kept at the peak of condition for the long periods of travel and storage necessary before it could be sold in the market? The ancient storage methods used for wheat, rice, corn, potatoes, yams, and beans consisted of harvesting them at maturity and storing them in a cool, dry place away from the light. They could then be preserved and shipped. In every case, the transportation of these foodstuffs was complex and costly and was only practiced on a large scale in time of famine.

A new preservation technique would make it possible to preserve freshly harvested fruit and vegetables in their natural state. In fact, consumers would be eating them fresh, even very fresh, thanks to refrigeration, a preservation technique that would keep them at a temperature a few degrees above freezing for the entire time before they were actually sold. This chilling would not be interrupted until the products were actually consumed. During transportation, while being stored and taken to be sold, and even while the foods were being kept at home before cooking, the maximum and minimum recommended temperatures must be maintained (for example between 43°F–50°F [6°C–10°C] for fruit and vegetables, between 36°F–39°F [2°C–4°C] for meat and fish). This keeps the cold chain going all the way through.

Today, the European grape—which originated in the southern Caucasus—is shipped from Chile to the northern hemisphere in winter, while green beans—South American plants—are flown from Kenya to Europe all year round. The wheel has come full circle for certain fruit such as peaches and pears, natives of China but grown for centuries throughout the temperate zones of the world. Now they are being exported from the world's newest orchards—which happen to be in China. Today, ginger, sesame seed, dried seaweed, lotus, okra, mangoes, lychees, mangosteens, rambutans, sweet potatoes, all ingredients that were once used exclusively in exotic cuisines, are available throughout the world.

A range of tropical vegetables and fruit can now be found in food stores, on restaurant menus, and on the dining table in private homes. Culinary tastes and habits have incorporated this produce, once synonymous with a particular season or a distant land, into their everyday diet. As they become more commonplace, the word "tropical" is being removed from official WHO documents governing the transportation of these fruit and vegetables, proof that they have become part of our daily life. People do not hesitate to cook them and will soon be eating them raw. As in the past, they are mixed in the preparation of dishes without regard to country of origin.

The introduction of freezing and chilling in the marketing of meat and fish has had the same effect. These foods can now be eaten raw, far from the ranch or the fishery. Hygiene regulations are constantly becoming stricter, and the reinforcement of legislation governing the raising of livestock will encourage consumers to try new approaches to uncooked food. However, like tartares (raw ground meat) and carpaccios (thinly sliced raw meat), raw fish and marinated raw fish require special vigilance in terms of their purchase, storage, and preparation if they are to be eaten safely (see the warning on page 173).

Why eat uncooked foods?

The Tsukiji fish market in Tokyo, where every day more than 2,300 tons of fresh fish, worth around 16 million US dollars, are sold.

Raw cuisines

The cold currents of the Pacific, such as the Humboldt current (which flows down the west coast of South America), or those that surround the islands of Japan and cool the waters of the northern Pacific Ocean, are very rich in fish. The countries near these fertile waters have given raw food cuisine its best recipes for fish. The inhabitants of the Pacific coastline continue to enjoy them. From Argentina to Mexico, seaside *cevicherias*—restaurants that specialize in marinated raw fish—line the beaches. The Japanese are the masters of sashimi, delicious morsels of raw fish, sometimes marinated but generally served completely uncooked and accompanied by soy sauce. The Polynesians, who live on the atolls of the Pacific, are also avid consumers of marinated raw fish.

The origins of seviche, the Latino marinated raw fish dish, can be traced back to pre-Columbian times, when raw fish was served with salt mixed with chili pepper and herbs. The introduction of citrus into the New World—and especially the lemon by the Spanish—produced a very sour marinade using freshly squeezed lemon juice, which was mixed with the condiments. The fish is diced or sliced into strips and immediately soaked in the marinade, which is later discarded. That is seviche as eaten today throughout the Americas and in Spanish-speaking communities elsewhere. It is usually consumed with ice-cold beer to quash the residual effects of *la leche de tigre (tiger's milk)*, which is the evocative name for the marinade.

Sashimi is really the art of slicing, because in this Japanese specialty the fish is worked in terms of textures, obtained on the basis of the type of cut used. There are seven ways of removing and slicing the fillets of fish into bite-sized portions. This quest for texture is also another way of producing subtle differences in the flavor of the fish. The technique of making sashimi dates back to the Nara dynasty (710–94), but it was not until the Edo dynasty (1600–1868) that it took on its current form. According to the Japanese, cold-water fish are best for producing sashimi. Today, the sashimi technique is even applied to the cutting and slicing of fruit and vegetables.

Salted duck breasts before drying
(see recipe page 64).

The Polynesians, those brave sailors and navigators famous for their epic journeys, explored all the islands of the Pacific ocean. Raw fish, which was so readily available and easy to prepare on board, is a dish in their culture that dates back to their original migrations. Shellfish is also consumed raw. Originally, the raw fish dish of the Hawaiian islands, known as *poke,* consisted of pieces of raw fish flavored with sea salt, onions, and seaweed. Later, after the Hawaiians had come into contact with Westerners, lime juice was added, as was coconut milk. Subsequently, the cuisines of Asian immigrants also influenced the ingredients in *poke,* which today consists of a mixture of raw fish, onions, chives, ginger, chili peppers, soy sauce, sesame oil, and salt.

Completely uncooked

It used to be the general rule that the only way in which meat and fish could safely be consumed was by cooking, salting, or drying, which were the only ways of killing the toxic bacteria that proliferated very quickly in the absence of freezing. It was known from experience that meat or fish had to be eaten cooked or salted, both to protect the eater from the effects of unsatisfactory preservation and to preserve them for as long as possible. The only way to eat these foods raw was by curing them first.

A recipe inspired
by Hawaiian cuisine
(see page 56).

The exception seems to have been the oyster, which has been eaten raw since antiquity and enjoyed in this way by all those who are familiar with it. In his *Grand Dictionnaire de Cuisine* (*Great Dictionary of Cooking*), Alexandre Dumas père notes that, as far as the Romans were concerned, "There was no such thing as a good dinner without raw oysters served on shaved ice." This has always meant procuring shellfish at the peak of freshness, like those set before the kings of France and the French court, which were brought from the Atlantic coast via the Loire River.

Why eat uncooked foods?

Nowadays, beef is the meat that is most frequently eaten raw, in the form of a tartare (ground meat) or a carpaccio (thinly sliced meat). Beef carpaccio owes its existence to a Venetian countess who, in the 1920s, became obsessed with a very particular diet. According to the dietetic diktat of the countess, beef had to be eaten raw. The only way to make it palatable was thus to serve it in very thin slices. According to those who enjoyed it, the brilliant hue of the raw meat was reminiscent of the treatment of reds in the work of the painter Carpaccio (1460–1525), whose work happened to be on show in a special exhibition in Venice at the time.

Salted and cured pork, which goes back to Roman times, is still highly prized. Italian and Spanish smoked and salted hams and pork belly continue to be the highlight of European *charcuterie*. There is also the so-called *viande des grisons* or *graubünden Fleisch,* which consists of air-dried goat or beef and is a Swiss delicacy. The Tuscan favorite, *lardo di Colonnata,* which is lard from pigs fed on acorns, is said to have an extraordinary flavor, but is more of a local specialty. In the past, many meat and fish were salted, dried, and pickled in barrels to serve as reserves for the winter or to feed ships' crews or troops on a campaign. The word "buccaneer" comes from *bucan*, a Carib word for smoked meat. The buccaneers of the sixteenth and seventeenth centuries hunted bison

In Europe, the everyday consumption of raw meat is a recent phenomenon, dating only from the twentieth century. The incident related by the aristocratic chronicler Pierre de Brantôme (1540–1614) concerning the voyage to Scotland of François de Vendôme (1519–45) may be symptomatic of the general approach to raw meat that existed in the past. In honor of their distinguished guest, the "savage Scots" organized a hunt of "red-haired and wild beasts," whose flesh was eaten raw, accompanied by pieces of bread, after being pressed with hazelnut sticks to extract the blood in an attempt to dry it. Brantôme notes that "among [the Scots] this was a very noble dish." According to Brantôme, Vendôme acquitted himself valiantly in his duties as the guest of honor, but did so without enthusiasm.[4]

on the larger islands of the West Indies to turn them into dried meat. *Bucan* thus became irrevocably linked with the pirates of the Caribbean, who bought buccaneer meat and who joined them in the raids that spread terror throughout the islands. Dried fish, such as herring and cod, were for centuries an important addition to the diet in the West. This is especially true of cod, which was caught in the Atlantic and the North Sea, salted, and shipped to the Mediterranean region. Salt cod is still an important ingredient in Portuguese cooking and in that of the west coast of France.

The Mediterranean has contributed several classic dishes to uncooked cuisine, such as the Spanish gazpacho, a chilled soup based on tomato; tzatziki (Greek) or cacik (Turkish), a cucumber and yogurt dip eaten in Greece, Turkey, and Cyprus. There are also the famous Mediterranean salads consisting of lettuce, arugula, or purslane, to which are added chervil, parsley, shredded cabbage, and chopped chives. Dill, an herb that immediately evokes Nordic cuisine, since it is found in so many Scandinavian dishes, may also be added.

Contemporary uncooked cuisine owes much to Scandinavian cooking. The famous gravlax is a dish of salmon marinated in dill, sugar, and salt (gravlax is a Swedish word derived from *gravad lax,* which means "buried salmon." Before the invention of refrigeration, the salmon was buried to keep it chilled.) Both this dish and the smorgasbord, which consists of an assortment of little canapés—including raw fish, uncooked fish roe, dried reindeer meat, or smoked eel—accompanied by raw vegetables, have been an inspiration for chefs worldwide. Another cuisine, this time originating from the Frozen North—Inuit cooking—uses several techniques for preparing raw food. The Inuit eat uncooked food fresh, frozen, dried, and fermented. Fermented meat is in fact meat whose fat is starting to putrefy. The flavor is much appreciated by the Inuit, and has been compared to that of Roquefort or other blue cheeses.

Uncooked cuisine requires impeccable hygiene.

Even if the skin is not to be eaten, fruit and vegetables should always be washed.

Hygiene when preparing uncooked food

When preparing uncooked food, everything must be kept impeccably clean and chilled. Wash and rinse cutting boards before and after each use, and wipe with a clean kitchen towel. Use different cutting and chopping boards depending on whether the food is of animal or vegetable origin. Once a week, the boards should be covered in coarse (kosher) salt and rinsed in boiling water. During the preparation of foods, a clean, damp sponge should be used to wipe the chopping board. Rinse and dry it between each use. Wash knife blades, and the handles as well, very carefully; keep blades very sharp. Meticulous cleaning of the hands, using a nailbrush, is essential, both during and after working in the kitchen.

Eggshells should be washed before breaking eggs, as should the skins of all vegetables and fruit, even if they are going to be discarded. You will need a set of machine-washable, plastic containers. Some, at least, should have the type of lid that can be vacuum-sealed. They will be needed constantly for refrigerating ingredients that have just been prepared before they can be arranged on the plate. The largest can be kept on the bottom shelf of the refrigerator and will be used for storing herbs and salad greens. These greens are first washed, cleaned, trimmed, and any faded or damaged leaves discarded. They should then be wrapped in damp, absorbent paper or paper towels. If prepared in this way, they will stay fresh for longer.

A last but absolutely vital precaution—maintain the cold chain at all times for any perishable foods that are to be served raw.

1. C. Lévi-Strauss, Didier Éribon, *De Près et de Loin* [From Near and Far] "Poche", Odile Jacob, 2001, p. 186.
2. C. Lévi-Strauss, Didier Éribon, *ibid.*, p. 187.
3. C. Lévi-Strauss, Didier Éribon, *ibid.*, p. 186.
4. A.-M. Cocula-Vaillières, *Brantôme: Amour et Gloire au Temps des Valois* [Brantôme: Love and Glory in the Days of the Dukes of Valois], Albin Michel, 1986, p. 97.

Damp absorbent paper and plastic wrap are required to preserve squash and zucchini blossoms for more than 24 hours.

Kitchen
techniques

Cutting

A Japanese mandoline, which is now widely available in Europe and the United States, is essential for cutting julienne strips or paper-thin slices from fruit and vegetables, and even from meat or fish. Meat and fish can only be sliced effectively if they are first semi-frozen.

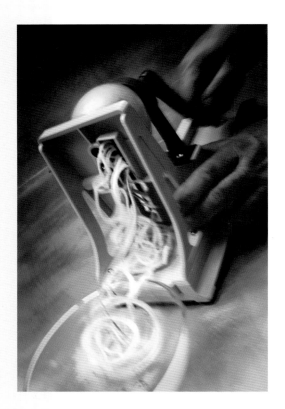

Milling

To make thin, spaghetti-like strands or ribbons of vegetables and fruit, only a French or Japanese vegetable mill will do.

Juicing

It is useful to have a dual citrus press and juicer for extracting the juices of fruit and vegetables.

Emulsifying

A hand-held mixer is an indispensable accessory for emulsifying and homogenizing sauces, as well as for blending fruit and vegetables, and making soups.

Grating

It is easy to grate the zest
from citrus fruit using a
good-quality hand-held grater.

Slicing

An electric slicer enables you to quickly and easily produce even slices from fruit,
vegetables, meat, and fish. In the case of meat and fish, you first need to leave them in
the freezer until they are semi-frozen.

Blending

This type of flask-
shaped blender is
vital for producing
smooth mixtures
in quantity—
a gazpacho, for
instance.

Mixing

If you want to produce the finest and thickest whipped cream, and beat egg
whites into stiff peaks, we recommend that you invest in the purchase of a
food mixer of this type. It has a robust whisking and beating attachment, and
can also be used as a processor, vegetable cutter, chopper, etc.

34
ingredients

and more than

100
recipes

Seaweed

Goat's cheese
with sea lettuce

1 | Divide goat's cheese into 4 equal portions. Roll these into balls in the palms of your hands.

2 | Chop the sea lettuce into small pieces and put it in a salad bowl. Add the cheese balls and roll them in the sea lettuce. When it comes into contact with the goat's cheese, the sea lettuce will rehydrate and delicately flavor the cheese.

3 | Cover a serving platter with plastic wrap and place the 4 balls on it. Refrigerate.

4 | Dissolve 2 pinches sea salt in the lime juice. Put all the ingredients for the dressing in a blender and process.

5 | To serve: spread 2 teaspoons of mango dressing on each of the chilled plates and place a cheese ball on top.

Goat's cheese with sea lettuce can accompany a fresh herb salad made with mint, tarragon, chervil, flat-leaved parsley, chives, lemon balm, oregano, etc.

Recommended wine:
Anjou Blanc 2002, Les Bergères (Jo Pithon).

Serves 4

7 oz (200 g) fresh
goat's cheese
Sea lettuce

Mango dressing
2 pinches sea salt
1 tablespoon lime juice
1 tablespoon sesame oil
2 tablespoons grape-
seed oil
3 tablespoons fresh
mango purée
Pepper

Salmon tartare and crunchy vegetables with sea lettuce and French mustard dressing

Serves 4

purple cauliflower
Romanesco broccoli
turnip
carrot
oz (15 g) rehydrated
sea lettuce
4 oz (400 g) salmon
rench mustard-flavored
vinegar
romaine lettuce leaves
6 chive flowers
ill

1 | Use 32 florets of purple cauliflower and 32 of the Romanesco broccoli, and dice the turnip and carrot into 32 small cubes. Chop the rehydrated sea lettuce. Dice the salmon into cubes whose sides measure ¼ inch (5 mm). Mix the ingredients together in a salad bowl.

2 | Blend the equivalent of a teaspoon of chopped sea lettuce with the French mustard dressing.

3 | Arrange the fish and vegetables in the center of four Romaine lettuce leaves. Sprinkle with a little dressing and pour a thin trail of sauce on one side. Scatter with chive flowers and dill.

Recommended wine: Patrimonio Blanc 2000, Grotta di Sole (Antoine Arena).

ALGAE. From the Latin *alga*. Algae live mainly in the sea, so most are commonly known as seaweed. They are a primitive plant without true leaves, stems, or roots, which grow in salt and fresh-water and in very damp places. The Japanese are the major consumers of seaweed, which they also cultivate and export. Algae have played an important role in the Japanese diet for over two thousand years. For this reason, edible seaweed is generally sold under its Japanese names, such as *kombu, wayang,* and *nori*. Of the 25,000 known species, only about fifty are edible. The texture, flavor, and nutritional value vary considerably from one seaweed to another, but all are rich in protein, minerals (calcium and iodine), and vitamins (A, B, and C). In view of their low fat and calorie content, seaweed is recommended for sufferers from arteriosclerosis, hypertension, obesity, and constipation.

Serves 4

4 passion fruit
1 sheet sea lettuce
12 scallops off the shell
Pepper

Scallop
carpaccio

1 | Scoop out the passion-fruit pulp into a sieve and press so that only the juice and pulp are retained. Set aside the seeds.

2 | Rehydrate the chopped algae in the passion-fruit juice and put aside.

3 | Clean the scallops, pat them dry, and place in the freezer for 30 minutes or until they are firm.

4 | Cut paper-thin slices from each scallop.

5 | Chill a plate and arrange 9 slices of scallop on each plate. Sprinkle with the algae-and-passion-fruit mixture and sprinkle a dozen of the fruit seeds over each plate.

Recommended wine: Condrieu 2002, Coteaux de Chéry (Georges Voinay).

Pineapple with brocciù cheese

1 | Chop the dried pineapple into ¼-inch (5-mm) cubes.

2 | Divide the Brocciù cheese into 4 equal portions. Roll each into a ball in the palm of your hands.

3 | Coat the balls with the dried pineapple by rolling them in it.

4 | Cover a plate with plastic wrap and arrange the 4 balls on it. Place in the refrigerator.

5 | Carefully peel the Victoria pineapple, core it, and cut 4 slices from it, each about ½ inch (1 cm) thick.

6 | Using a piping syringe, on each plate trace 5 lines of balsamic vinegar and 5 parallel lines of pistachio oil. Arrange 1 slice of pineapple and 1 ball of Brocciù cheese on the lines. Season.

Recommended wine: Vouvray Demi-Sec 1996, Domaine Vhet-le-Mont (Noël Pinguet).

Serves 4

4 dried pineapple rings
7 oz (200 g) Brocciù cheese
1 fresh Victoria pineapple
Balsamic vinegar
Pistachio oil
Pepper and sea salt

PINEAPPLE This plant originated in the American tropics, Central America, and the Caribbean, where it was cultivated two thousand years ago for its large fruit and sweet, tasty flesh. In 1493, Christopher Columbus brought pineapple back to Europe from a voyage to Guadeloupe, but it became clear that the plant would not survive in temperate latitudes. Shortly afterward, the Portuguese and Spanish introduced it to the Asian colonies. Wealthy northern Europeans built special hothouses in which to cultivate pineapples for the table before refrigeration made it possible to import them from the tropics. The pineapple is now cultivated for export in its area of origin, as well as in subtropical Australia and the Pacific Islands. Pineapples are exported mainly from Hawaii and Côte d'Ivoire to the United States and Western Europe respectively. The pineapple, so called because its skin resembles that of a pine cone, is rich in vitamin C, potassium, folic acid, and magnesium. It has diuretic properties, eliminates toxins, and the enzymes it contains facilitate the digestion of protein.

Serves 4

2 duck breasts
1 Victoria pineapple
2 tablespoons
  chopped purple basil
1 small fresh red chili
  pepper, chopped
12 mint leaves, chopped
1 lime
4 teaspoons maple syrup
1 tablespoon
  balsamic vinegar
1 tablespoon soy sauce
1 teaspoon
  fresh grated ginger
Freshly ground black
  pepper
2 tablespoons sesame oil
1 tablespoon
  fennel fronds
4 quails' eggs
4 dried pineapple rings
Red pepper or 3 drops
  Tabasco sauce

Sweet-and-sour duck tartare with pineapple

1 | Trim the fat from the duck breast and cut it into ¼-inch (5-mm) cubes. Carefully peel the pineapple and cut it into cubes of identical size.

2 | In a large bowl, combine the duck breast, pineapple, chopped purple basil, chopped chili pepper, chopped mint, lime juice, 2 teaspoons maple syrup, balsamic vinegar, soy sauce, ginger, black pepper, and sesame oil.

3 | Place a square mold on a plate and fill it with the tartare. Remove the mold.

4 | Arrange a few fennel fronds on top. Slice off the top of a quail's egg and place the egg carefully in the center of the arrangement, as if in a nest. Arrange half a round of dried pineapple vertically behind it. Surround the whole with a trail of maple syrup.

Recommended wine:
Tavel 2002, Mas de l'Anglore (Éric Pfifferling).

Pineapple tabbouleh

1 | Make the sauce the night before by blending the raspberries and sugar for at least a minute. Strain the sauce over a bowl. Refrigerate until required.

2 | On the day of serving, combine the olive oil and lemon juice in a large bowl. Season with pepper.

3 | Sprinkle this with the couscous grains. Fold in lightly and leave to swell for 30 minutes, stirring occasionally.

4 | Carefully peel the pineapple and cut it into ¼-inch (5-mm) cubes.

5 | To the couscous, add the diced pineapple, chopped mint, chopped coriander, and lime zest. Mix well.

6 | To assemble the dish, take a cocktail glass and first pour in 1 tablespoon raspberry sauce, then cover with the pineapple tabbouleh. Decorate with an edible flower, such as a violet.

NB: If the raspberry sauce is too thick, add a little cold water and beat with a whisk.

Recommended wine: Vouvray Moelleux AOC 2002, La Ferme (Lemaire-Fournier).

Serves 4

8 oz (250 g) raspberries
¼ cup (50 g) sugar
4 tablespoons extra-virgin olive oil
Juice of 2 lemons
Pepper
7 oz (200 g) medium couscous
1 fresh Victoria pineapple
6 mint leaves, chopped
2 tablespoons chopped coriander
Zest of 1 lime

Creamy asparagus soup

1 | Wash and peel the asparagus. Break off and discard the woody lower 1½ inches (4 cm) or so of the stalks.

2 | Set aside 2 of the asparagus, and slice them on a mandoline to obtain shavings.

3 | In a blender, combine all the other ingredients at maximum speed. Strain through a conical sieve and season to taste. Divide between 4 bowls and arrange 3 asparagus shavings per bowl. Sprinkle with a few drops of extra-virgin olive oil. Serve immediately.

Recommended wine:
Arbois-Pupillin 1998
(Emmanuel Houillon).

Serves 4

16 asparagus spears
½ avocado, peeled
  and chopped
1 cup mineral water
1 teaspoon chopped celery
2 tablespoons extra-virgin
  olive oil
2 teaspoons lemon juice
1 pinch Espelette chili
  pepper
1 teaspoon chopped
  onion
1 teaspoon chopped
  garlic
2 teaspoons chopped
  tarragon
Sea salt and black pepper

Asparagus strips and cured duck with herb salad

Serves 4

20 thin slices cured duck
  (see recipe page 64)
20 baby green asparagus
  spears
2 tablespoons hazelnut oil
1 teaspoon balsamic
  vinegar
Salt and pepper

Herb Salad
Arugula
Chive flowers
Tarragon
Chervil

1 | Using an electric carving knife or very sharp kitchen knife, slice the duck into 20 very thin slices.

2 | Roll each asparagus spear in a slice of duck.

3 | Blend the hazelnut oil and balsamic vinegar in a food processor or blender. Season to taste.

4 | Arrange a mound of salad herbs and place the wrapped asparagus spears in front of it. Sprinkle carefully with the sauce.

Recommended wine:
Meursault Premier Cru 1997, Les Charmes (Vincent Girardin).

ASPARAGUS, from the Latin *asparagus*, itself from the Greek *asparagos* meaning "shoot." The asparagus is a noble vegetable that has been eaten for two thousand years. It was enjoyed by the peoples of antiquity from Egypt to Rome, including Greece, and was noted for its medicinal properties. It fell into oblivion in the Middle Ages, but was revived at the table of King Louis XIV of France, who restored its noble credentials. The king's agronomist, Jean de La Quintinie, was the first to cultivate asparagus out of season. Its intensive cultivation in France dates back to the early nineteenth century. Asparagus is an excellent source of folic acid, and also contains potassium, vitamins A, B_6, and C, copper, iron, phosphorus, and zinc. Asparagus has strong diuretic properties, but is not generally recommended in this regard due to its irritant effect on those with kidney problems and on people with a sensitive urinary tract.

Serves 4

8 white asparagus spears
2 limes
1 chili pepper
7 oz (250 g) salmon
   steak
4 teaspoons avocado oil
2 passion fruit
Salt and pepper
Borage flower (to
   contribute an oyster-
   like flavor)

Asparagus strands, salmon tartare, passion fruit, and borage flower

1 | Wash and peel the asparagus. Break off the bottom 1½ inches (4 cm) or so of stem and discard. Starting with the stem end, slice the tips one by one on a Japanese mandoline fitted with fine blades. Set aside these asparagus strands in a bowl of iced water.

2 | Peel 1 lime, discarding the pith. Cut it into 4 quarters. Chop the chili pepper.

3 | Cut the salmon into ½-inch (1-cm) cubes. In a bowl, combine the lime, chili pepper, avocado oil, passion fruit, salt, and pepper with the salmon.

4 | Pat the asparagus strips dry with a paper towel. Put them in a bowl and sprinkle them with 2 teaspoons avocado oil and the zest of the second lime.

5 | On chilled plates, arrange a mound of asparagus strands about 4 inches (10 cm) in diameter. Sprinkle with 1 tablespoon salmon cubes. Top with a borage flower. Serve immediately.

Recommended wine: Beaune Premier Cru Blanc 1999, Les Coucherias (Jean-Claude Rateau).

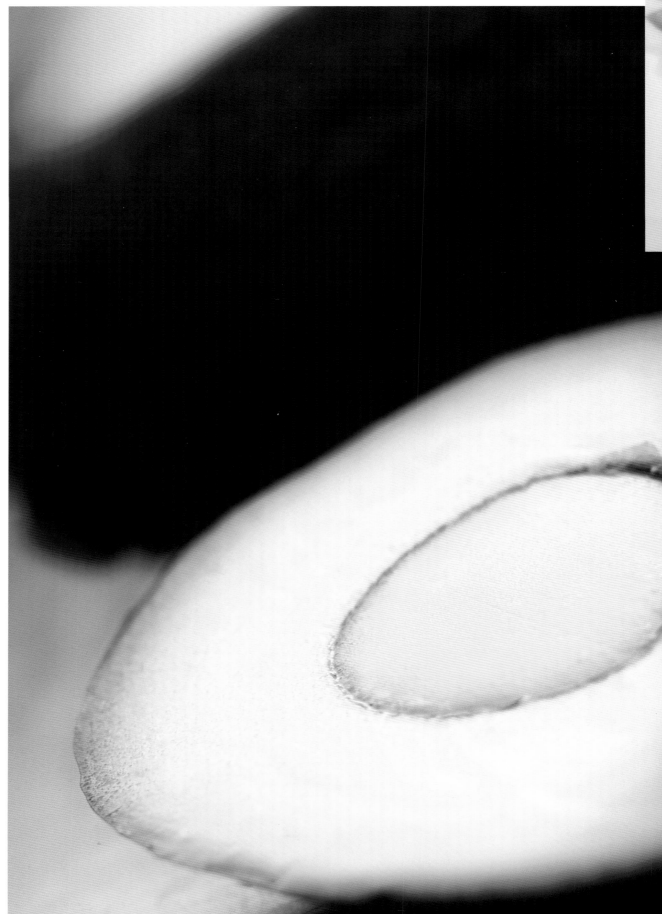

Avocado

AVOCADO. from the Spanish *abogado*, and the Aztec *auacatl*. Pear-shaped fruit that can grow to a weight of 2 lbs (1 kg), of which there are a dozen common varieties. The strongly scented flowers of the tree are yellow, white, and green. The fruit originated in from Central America, where it has been eaten for centuries. The first Spanish explorers noted that it was cultivated in Mexico and Peru. It has only become popular in Europe and North America since the end of World War II. The avocado has considerable nutritional properties. Thanks to its potassium, folic acid, vitamins A, B_6, and C, and magnesium, the avocado is a fruit that supplies energy. Despite its high fat content, it is easily digestible because it contains numerous enzymes that facilitate the absorption of fat. It is thus recommended for digestive disorders. Some varieties have a rough skin and for this reason the fruit is also known as an alligator pear.

Variations on guacamole

1 | Process the avocados with the lime juice, chopped onion, fresh coriander, water, salt, and pepper. Cover with plastic wrap and place in the refrigerator.

2 | Use a mandoline to slice 12 ribbons of daikon about 6 inches (15 cm) long and 2 inches (5 cm) wide. Steep them in a bowl of iced water.

3 | Cut the baby corn into rounds.

4 | On a rectangular plate, arrange two lines of the avocado purée, 3 ribbons of daikon, 7 slices of corn, 5 purslane leaves, 1 beet leaf stem sliced into 7, and 3 zucchini blossom pistils. Delicately sprinkle with the two oils.

Recommended wine: Beaujolais Blanc 2000, Domaine des Terres-Dorées (J.-P. Brun).

Serves 4

2 avocados
1 tablespoon lime juice
2 teaspoons chopped onion
3 teaspoons fresh coriander
½ cup mineral water
Salt and pepper
1 daikon or black radish
4 ears of baby corn
20 purslane leaves
4 beet leaves
12 zucchini blossom pistils
1 tablespoon avocado oil
1 tablespoon argan oil

Creamed avocado
with osetra caviar

Blend all the ingredients, except the caviar, in a blender on maximum speed. Distribute the creamed avocado mixture among 4 small bowls and top each with 1 teaspoon of caviar.

Recommended wine: Jurançon Sec 2002, Domaine Cauhape.

Serves 4

4 avocados
Juice of 1 lime
Sea salt
Freshly ground pepper
4 teaspoons Osetra caviar

Serves 4

1 pomelo
2 green apples
Juice of 1 lemon
4 avocados
10 mint leaves
1 tablespoon chopped
   fennel fronds
2 tablespoons avocado oil
1 teaspoon mango
   vinegar

Avocado and
pomelo tartare

1 | Peel the pomelo, discarding the pith. Cut each segment into three. Refrigerate until required.

2 | Use a mandoline to slice 12 thin apple rings from the thickest part of both apples. Sprinkle with lemon juice, cover with plastic wrap and refrigerate until required.

3 | Use a melon baller to cut out 24 small balls from the avocados. Sprinkle with lemon juice, cover with plastic wrap and refrigerate until required.

4 | Chop the mint. In a blender, combine the chopped fennel, avocado oil, and mango vinegar.

5 | In a large bowl, mix the pomelo and avocado with the dressing and the chopped mint.

6 | On a chilled plate, arrange a round of green apple, then a ball of avocado and a segment of pomelo. Top with a slice of green apple and arrange the fruit in layers, ending with a round of apple. Place an avocado ball on top and garnish with fennel fronds.

Recommended wine: Aligoté Burgundy 2001, Domaine Auber-et-Paméla-de-Villaine.

Banana

BANANA from the Portuguese *banana*, probably a word of Bantu origin, from Guinea in central Africa. The banana shrub developed in the tropics and subtropics and produces its fruit in large bunches called "hands." After annual fruiting, the fruit part dries up and is replaced by a new shoot. The banana is believed to have originally appeared in Malaysia millions of years ago, but it is first documented as growing in India in the sixth and fifth centuries BCE. An Indian version of Genesis makes it the Fruit of Knowledge offered to Adam by Eve, which is why in India it is known as the "fruit of paradise." As it ripens, the sugars in the banana are converted from starch, which is difficult to digest, to sugars—such as fructose and glucose—that can be easily absorbed. The banana is a good source of vitamins B_6 and C, potassium, folic acid, and magnesium.

1 | Make the iced meringue the night before. Beat the egg whites into stiff peaks. Split the vanilla beans and scrape out the pulp and seeds, and mix them with the egg whites and confectioner's sugar. Place in the freezer.

2 | On the day itself, cut off the top of the banana at an angle and slice the bottom horizontally. Remove the flesh, keeping the peel intact, and purée the flesh in a blender. Add the sugar, and sprinkle with a few drops of lemon juice. Strain through a conical sieve. Refrigerate until required.

3 | Carefully cut the passion fruit in half, keeping the skins whole. Scoop out the pulp and seeds into a small bowl and refrigerate until required.

Open avocado ravioli, banana
and ginger compote, with maple syrup

1 | Use a mandoline to slice whole, unpeeled avocados, so as to obtain 8 slices that are as large as possible. Cover the slices of avocado with lemon juice.

2 | Mash the bananas with a fork. Mix them with 1 teaspoon grated ginger, 1 pinch of salt, 2 teaspoons sugar, and 2 teaspoons lime juice.

3 | On a plate, arrange 1 slice avocado, and garnish the widest part with a scant tablespoon of the banana-and-ginger mixture. Cover with a second slice of avocado in order to obtain a sort of open ravioli. On one side, add 1 teaspoon of maple syrup, and sprinkle a few chopped pistachios next to this.

Recommended wine: Riesling 1998, Cuvée Frédéric-Émile-Trimbach.

Serves 4

4 avocados
Juice of 1 lemon
2 bananas
1 teaspoon grated fresh
  ginger root
1 pinch of salt
2 teaspoons sugar
Juice of ½ lime
4 teaspoons maple syrup
2 tablespoons chopped
  pistachios

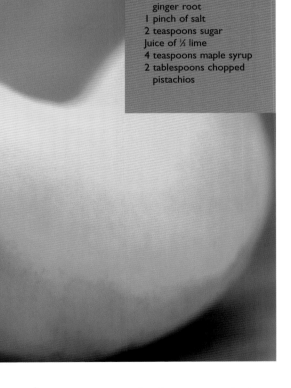

Banana à la banane,
iced meringue,
and passion-fruit juice

4 | Arrange 4 scoops of iced meringue in the 4 passion-fruit shells. Freeze until required.

5 | Whip the cream and fold it into the banana purée. Fill the banana skins with the mixture.

6 | Arrange 1 banana skin and half a filled passion-fruit shell on a plate. Sprinkle the meringue with passion-fruit pulp before serving.

Recommended wine: Muscat de Beaumes-de-Venise.

Serves 4

Iced Meringue
8 egg whites
2 vanilla beans
¼ cup confectioner's sugar

4 bananas
1½ tablespoons sugar
A few drops
  of lemon juice
3 passion fruit
7 fl oz (200 ml) light
  whipping cream

Serves 4

2 mackerel
2 tablespoons 15-year-old
   balsamic vinegar
2 bananas
Juice of 1 lemon
2 teaspoons coriander
   seeds
8 Chinese green onion
   (scallion) strands
Salt and pepper

Glazed mackerel
with balsamic vinegar, banana chips, and coriander

1 | Fillet the mackerels, skin them and remove any remaining bones
with tweezers. Wash the fillets and pat them very dry. Use a brush
to glaze the fillets with balsamic vinegar. Cover a plate with plastic
wrap and arrange the fillets on it.

2 | Slice the bananas into rounds ⅛ inch (3 mm) thick. Sprinkle them
with lemon juice.

3 | Arrange the fillets on plates, cover them lengthwise with banana
slices, and sprinkle with crushed coriander seeds. Arrange a
Chinese green onion (scallion) strand on each side.

Recommended wine: Saint-Chinian Rouge 1998, Château
Soulié-des-Joncs.

Bass

Carpaccio of sea bass, kiwi fruit, bottarga, and lime

1 | Freeze the bass fillets for half an hour before use. Then slice them into thin slices, around ¹⁄₁₆ inch (2 mm) thick. Arrange the raw bass slices on plates rinsed under cold running water.

2 | To each plate add ½ a kiwi fruit cut into cubes, 2 chopped shiso leaves, and a dozen shavings of bottarga. Add a thin strip of lime, and season with salt and pepper. Serve immediately.

Recommended wine: White Vin de Pays des Bouches-du-Rhône 1999, Domaine Hauvette.

Serves 4

4 wild bass fillets
2 kiwi fruit
8 shiso leaves
1 bottarga
1 lime
Salt and pepper

Serves 4

7 fl oz (200 ml) squid ink
2 oysters
4 small bass fillets, boned
Olive oil
2 limes
1½ oz (40 g) peanuts
Tabasco sauce
Sea salt and pepper
4 small eggs
1 oz (30 g) marsh samphire
1 small red onion

Bass tartare

BASS from Middle German *baerse, barse,* a word used to designate several fish, including perch and bass. Bass is also known in English as sea bass and in French as *loup de mer* (sea wolf), especially in the south. It is a voracious predator with a long head and large mouth that remains open as it swims, so that it can swallow anything in its path, in a feeding frenzy. This means that its prey is varied, consisting of smaller creatures such as sardines, anchovies, squid, and crustaceans. The flesh is fine, firm and with a delicious, delicate flavor that is highly sought after by gourmets. Bass is very easily suited to farming, and aquaculture does nothing to spoil its nutritional qualities. It is a lean fish containing less than 5% fat. It is rich in protein and omega 3s (which combat cholesterol).

1 | Dilute the squid or octopus ink with the lemon juice and liquid from the oysters. Season if necessary.

2 | Fillet the bass and dice the flesh into small ¼-inch (5-mm) cubes. Transfer to a bowl and sprinkle with the olive oil, lime juice, peanuts, Tabasco sauce, salt, and pepper.

3 | Arrange the tartare on each plate, using a small square mold. On top arrange an egg yolk, a few strands of marsh samphire, and some thin slices of red onion. Use a piping syringe or bag, remove half the egg yolk and replace it with the same quantity of the squid-ink and oyster preparation.

Recommended wine: Condrieu.

Bass and green zebra tartare, with coconut foam and passion fruit

1 | Dice the bass and Green Zebra tomatoes. Mix them in a salad bowl with chive flowers. Season with olive oil, lime juice, salt, and chili pepper.

2 | Pour the coconut milk into a blender and process until it foams.

3 | Rinse a plate with cold water, place a 4-inch (10-cm) diameter hoop on it, and fill it with the bass tartare. Place a ring of coconut foam around the tartare and sprinke with a few passion-fruit seeds. Complete the garnish with a borage flower.

Recommended wine: Côtes-du-Jura Blanc 1998, Domaine Claude-Charbonnier.

Serves 4

4 wild bass fillets
4 Green Zebra tomatoes
20 chive flowers
1 tablespoon olive oil
1 tablespoon lime juice
Salt
1 chili pepper
1 cup (250 ml) unsweetened
    coconut milk
2 passion fruit
4 borage flowers

Beet ravioli,
green zebra soup,
and sprouted seeds

1 | In a bowl, mix the fresh goat's cheese and chopped chives. Season with salt, pepper, and a tablespoon of olive oil. Cover with plastic wrap and refrigerate until required.

2 | In a blender or food processor, combine 4 tomatoes with the white balsamic vinegar. Season with salt and refrigerate until required.

3 | Peel the beets and slice them into 32 thin slices. Spread a sheet of plastic wrap over the work surface, place the beet slices on it, and brush them with olive oil. Turn them over and in the center of each slice place a teaspoon of goat's cheese. Cover with a second slice of beet, and pinch round the edges, in order to obtain circular beet ravioli.

4 | Deseed the remaining tomato and slice it into ¼-inch (5-mm) slices.

5 | Cover the bottom of a soup plate with the Green Zebra tomato slices and arrange 4 beet ravioli on top. Sprinkle with a bit of the diced green tomato, some cumin seeds, beet sprouts, and salt.

Recommended wine: Mâcon-Bussières, Domaine de la Sarazinière.

Veal carpaccio
with beet purée and wasabi

Serves 4

9 oz (250 g) lean veal
1 beet
8 fl oz (250 ml) extra
   virgin olive oil
12 capers
Wasabi
Sea salt

1 | Place the veal in the freezer for 30 minutes.

2 | Peel the beet and process it in a food processor. Pour the oil in a stream over the beet juice (as if making a mayonnaise). Refrigerate until required.

3 | Using an electric slicer or very sharp knife, slice the veal into the thinnest possible slices.

4 | Arrange the slices on a plate rinsed under cold water. Place a dab of mayonnaise next to it. Finish by topping the veal with three capers, a dab of wasabi, and a pinch of sea salt. Serve immediately.

Recommended wine: White Coteaux-du-Languedoc 2001, Domaine de l'Hortus.

Beet

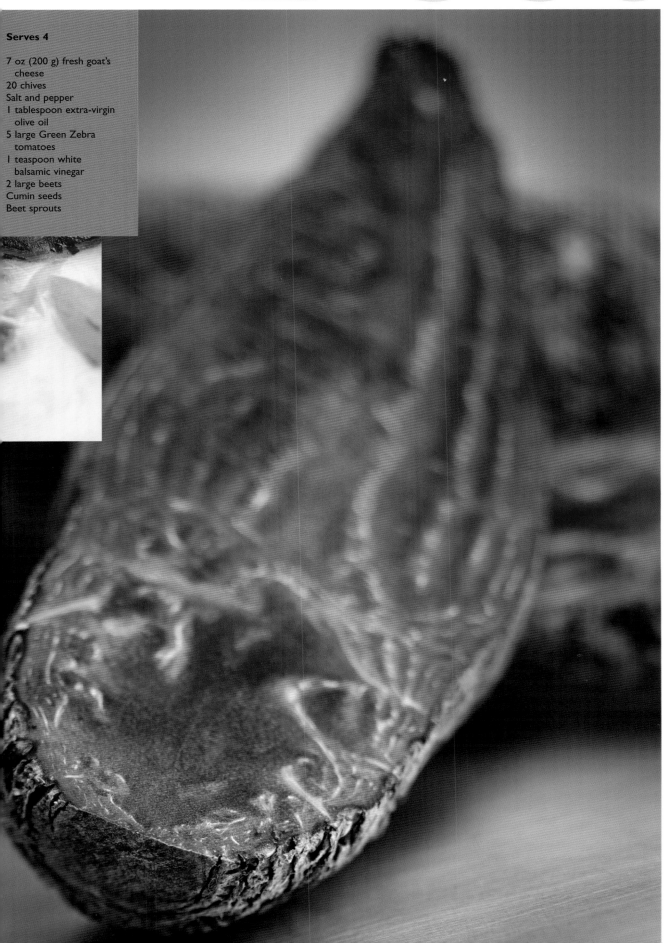

Serves 4

7 oz (200 g) fresh goat's
  cheese
20 chives
Salt and pepper
1 tablespoon extra-virgin
  olive oil
5 large Green Zebra
  tomatoes
1 teaspoon white
  balsamic vinegar
2 large beets
Cumin seeds
Beet sprouts

BEET, from the Latin *beta* "garden vegetable with large leaves and ribs." Beet (*beta vulgaris*) is a European biennial plant with a taproot; there are four varieties. One variety, the mangelwurzel, is used as animal fodder; another, the sugar beet, is grown for the sugar in its roots. The third variety is Swiss chard, also known as silver beet, a plant with fleshy ribs. All these types were known to the Greeks and Romans, although the fleshy taproot of the beet was developed through cultivation in the Middle Ages until it became as large as it is today. The beet gets its distinctive dark red coloring from the combination of two pigments, betacyanin and betaxanthin. Beet is an excellent source of potassium and vitamin A, and also contains trace elements of magnesium, vitamin C, iron, copper, calcium, folic acid, and zinc. It is easily digested and stimulates the appetite. It is said to cure headaches, head colds, and anemia.

Serves 4

12 scallops
1 large beet
Hazelnut oil
Salt
1 teaspoon balsamic
 vinegar
2 tablespoons pistachio
 oil
1 teaspoon soy sauce
1 bunch coriander
 flowers

Scallop carpaccio
and beet spaghettini
with pistachio dressing

1 | Clean the scallops and place them in the freezer.

2 | Using a mandoline with thin blades or a shredder, shred the beet into spaghetti-type strands. Arrange them in a salad bowl and sprinkle with hazelnut oil. Cover with plastic wrap and set aside.

3 | Dissolve a pinch of salt in the balsamic vinegar. In a blender, combine the pistachio oil, vinegar, and soy sauce.

4 | Slice each scallop into 3 rounds.

5 | Make a nest of the beet spaghettini in the center of the plate. Arrange the scallop rounds on it, and pour a thin trace of the dressing around it. Complete with coriander flowers.

Recommended wine: Riesling Grand Cru 2000, Kastelberg, Domaine Kreydenweiss.

Duck

DUCK, a web-footed aquatic bird. Its flattened beak enables it to filter the silt at the bottom of fresh-water pools and rivers, from which it obtains vegetable matter and small prey. The word is old English and is of the same origin as the verb "to duck," referring to the bird's habit of lowering its head and disappearing under water. Wild ducks migrate, but domesticated ducks do not. The duck was first domesticated about four thousand years ago in China. This long shared history allowed the Chinese to observe that ducks, who live in pairs, "went into mourning" if one of the pair died, and they thus became the symbol of fidelity. Several species of duck are bred in Europe, especially in France, to satisfy the demand for foie gras. There are around eighty different breeds of duck, all of which have slightly different nutritional properties. Whether they are wild or tame also has a bearing—the raw flesh of the wild duck contains approximately 30 percent less fat than domesticated species. All duck meat is rich in iron and vitamin B.

Duck seviche
with wild berries

Serves 4

2 duck breasts
1 bird's-eye chili pepper
1 red bell pepper
4 sprigs chervil
20 white currants
20 redcurrants
12 blackberries
12 blackcurrants
Juice of 2 oranges
Juice of 1 lime
4 violet flowers

1 | Dice the duck meat into small cubes and refrigerate until required.

2 | Chop the chili pepper, and slice the bell pepper into thin slices on a mandoline. Chop three sprigs of chervil.

3 | In a salad bowl, combine all the ingredients except for 1 chervil sprig and the violet flowers.

4 | Arrange glass bowls on a bed of ice cubes, and sprinkle them with the duck seviche.

5 | Garnish with the reserved chervil sprig and 1 violet flower.

Recommended wine : Corbières Rouge 1999, Cuvée Respect de la Nature, Château Coulon.

Serves 4

1 large duck breast
8 dried prunes
Small spinach leaves
Tarragon
Chervil
Coriander flowers
Fennel seeds
Extra-virgin olive oil

Duck carpaccio with prune coating and contrasting salad

1 | Put the duck breast in the freezer for 30 minutes.

2 | In a coffee mill, grind the dried prunes to a powder.

3 | Make a salad with the spinach, tarragon, chervil, coriander flowers, and fennel seeds. Season with a little olive oil.

4 | Using an electric knife or a very sharp kitchen knife, slice the breast into 48 paper-thin slices.

5 | On a chilled plate, shape the duck carpaccio into a square. Sprinkle the inside of a square cookie cutter or mold, smaller than the carpaccio, with the ground prunes. Arrange a mound of salad on one side.

Recommended wine: Riesling Late Harvest 1998, Rot Murle (Pierre Trick).

Cured
duck

1 | In a small bowl, combine the coarse salt and chopped thyme. Crush the bay leaves in a mortar and add them to the bowl with the sugar, coriander seeds, and pepper. Mince the garlic clove. Remove half of the fat from the skin of the duck breast. Take a piece of plastic wrap measuring 12 x 16 inches (30 x 40 cm). In the center, spread out half the seasoned salt and the garlic to cover an area the same size as the breast. Place the breast on it, skin downward. Cover with the rest of the salt and the garlic. Wrap the plastic wrap tightly over the the top. Transfer to a plate and leave in the lower part of the refrigerator for 4 days.

2 | Remove from the refrigerator after 4 days, and take the duck out of the plastic wrap. Rinse it well and pat dry. Wrap it tightly in burlap used for curing ham and truss it. Suspend it in the bottom of the refrigerator or, better still, in a cool, well-ventilated cellar.

3 | Eat 3 weeks later.

Recommended wine: Morgon AOC 2002, Côte de Py (Jean Foillard).

Serves 4

Prepare 1 month before serving
1 large duck breast, with skin
14 oz (400 g) coarse
   gray salt
1 tablespoon chopped thyme
2 bay leaves
½ cup sugar
2 teaspoons coriander seeds
Pepper
1 garlic clove

Mushroom

Enoki, cured duck, and black radish, tortilla-style

1 | Purée the mango half. Sprinkle it with lemon juice and set aside in a cool place.

2 | Using a mandoline, slice the black radish into 12 thin slices.

3 | Separate the bunch of enoki mushrooms into 12. Make 12 enoki cones with 1 slice black radish, 1 slice duck, and 1 chive.

4 | On a plate, preferably one that is dark in color, arrange 3 cones, drawing a line of balsamic vinegar between each. On this line, place 1 teaspoon of mango purée. Repeat for the other 3 plates.

Recommended wine: Burgundy AOC 2001 (Fred Cossard).

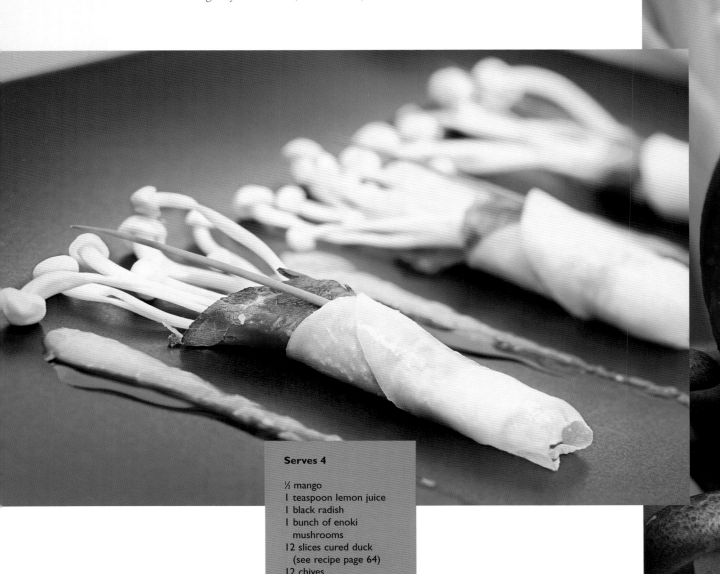

Serves 4

½ mango
1 teaspoon lemon juice
1 black radish
1 bunch of enoki
 mushrooms
12 slices cured duck
 (see recipe page 64)
12 chives
Balsamic vinegar

Serves 4

1 tablespoon balsamic
  vinegar
Sea salt
2 tablespoons peanut oil
1 tablespoon chopped
  flat-leaved parsley
32 shiitake mushrooms
12 baby green asparagus
4 rounds fresh lotus root
48 enoki mushrooms

Mushrooms, asparagus, lotus, and peanut sauce

1 | Dissolve the salt in the balsamic vinegar. Process it
with the peanut oil and chopped parsley.

2 | In the center of each plate, arrange 8 shiitake
mushrooms. Slip 3 baby green asparagus sprears
into the holes of a piece of lotus root and place it on
top. Pour a little of the dressing over and around the
vegetables. Complete the garnish by arranging 12
enoki mushrooms around the shiitake.

Recommended wine: Tokay Pinot Gris 1999,
Cuvée de l'Ours (Charles Frey).

MUSHROOM The mushroom is a fungus. Fungi are now classified in
a separate kingdom from all other plants since they possess none of the
characteristics of other plants: they have no stem, root, veins, leaves,
flowers, or fruit. They do not contain chlorophyll and have to borrow
carbons from other organisms or draw them from inert substances. About
30 species out of the 200,000 or so fungi are cultivated in various parts
of the world, but only very few species are sold commercially. Shiitake
(*Lentinus edodes*) is an Asian species that grows on the dead trunks of several
species of tree in mountain forests. It has been eaten for more than two
thousand years, occupying a similar niche in Japanese cuisine to that of the
store mushroom in Europe. It is said to lower blood pressure and to help
fight influenza, tumors, stomach ulcers, and diabetes. Shiitake are sold fresh
as well as dry and are reasonably easy to find in the West.

Consommé of shiitake mushrooms, cucumber, and chive flowers

1 | Soak the shiitake in water.

2 | Use a mandoline to produce 20 paper-thin cucumber slices.

3 | Line a sieve with cheesecloth and filter the mushroom water into a salad bowl. Cut the mushrooms into slices.

4 | In each serving bowl, arrange 5 cucumber slices and 7 mushroom slices. Cover with the mushroom liquid. Season with salt and pepper and sprinkle with a few chopped chives and the 7 chive flowers.

Serves 4

8 oz (250 g) dried shiitake
  mushrooms
8 fl oz (250 ml) filtered water
1 cucumber
Salt and pepper
12 chive sprigs
28 chive flowers

Cauliflower

Serves 4

1 cauliflower
2 tablespoons chopped
  beets
2 tablespoons chopped
  pitchouline olives
20 tarragon leaves,
  chopped
2 tablespoons avocado oil
1 teaspoon balsamic
  vinegar
Daikon sprouts
Fennel fronds

CAULIFLOWER, from the Latin *caulis* meaning "stem" and *flor* meaning "flower." A biennial and even triennial hardy plant that grows wild on both sides of the Atlantic, as well as in the Mediterranean, and in Western and Southern Europe. The plant has been domesticated since Neolithic times, and several thousand years of cultivation and selection have produced varieties and strains so different that it is hard to believe they have a common ancestor. The cabbage, from which the cauliflower derives, was known to the Greeks and Romans, and is probably of Italian origin. At the court of King Louis XIV of France it was considered to be something of a novelty. Its very high water content means the cauliflower is low in calories. However, it does contain vitamin C and was reputedly effective against scurvy.

Oysters in purple cauliflower batter and whipped cream with horseradish

1 | Whip the cream until stiff. Fold in the horseradish and refrigerate until required.

2 | Open the oysters. Remove them from the shells and place them in a large bowl on a bed of ice.

3 | Grate the tips of the cauliflower florets. You want enough cauliflower "breadcrumbs" to roll the oysters in.

4 | Pour 1 cup coarse salt into the center of each plate. Wash and dry the oyster shells and arrange them in the plate. Drop a large dab of the whipped cream in each oyster shell. Top with 1 "breaded" oyster and garnish each with 3 chives.

Recommended wine: Corbières Blanc 1998, Cuvée Prestige, Château de Caraguilmes.

Serves 4

7 fl oz (200 ml) whipping cream
2 teaspoons grated horseradish
12 G2 oysters
1 purple cauliflower
4 cups coarse sea salt
12 chives

Cauliflower tabbouleh

1 | Grate the cauliflower to obtain tiny pieces the size of couscous. Mix with the beet, olives, and chopped tarragon. Sprinkle with avocado oil and balsamic vinegar. Season with salt and pepper.

2 | Place a 4-inch (10-cm) diameter hoop in the center of a plate. Fill it with the cauliflower tabbouleh. Surround it with a trail of avocado oil and balsamic vinegar. Arrange a few daikon sprouts alternately with a few fennel fronds around the mound.

Recommended wine: Gewürztraminer 1999 (Charles Frey).

Serves 4

1 sweet onion
Aged wine vinegar
1 cauliflower
3 tablespoons
  unsweetened coconut
  milk
Salt and pepper
20 red orach or young
  spinach leaves
Extra-virgin olive oil

Creamed cauliflower, red orach, and marinated onion rings

1 | Slice the onion on a mandoline in order to obtain 20 thin slices. Leave them to marinate for 2 hours in the aged wine vinegar.

2 | Process the cauliflower in a blender with the coconut milk and a little water until the mixture is a smooth cream. Season with salt and pepper.

3 | Fill serving bowls with the cauliflower cream. Drain the onion slices. Arrange 5 red orach leaves and 5 onion slices in the soup and finish with a few drops of olive oil.

Recommended wine: Tokay Pinot Gris 1999, Cuvée de l'Ours (Charles Frey).

Serves 4

2 cucumbers
1 lb 5 oz (600 g) fragrant
    strawberries
1 teaspoon sugar crystals
Salt and pepper
12 black olives
2 tablespoons extra
    virgin olive oil
1 tablespoon sherry
    vinegar
8 large green basil leaves,
    finely chopped

Cucumber spaghetti, strawberry juice, and crushed olives

1 | Use a vegetable mill to slice the cucumbers into spaghetti-like strands.

2 | Hull and wash the strawberries. Process them in a blender with the sugar and season with salt and pepper.

3 | Chop the olives.

4 | In a salad bowl, combine the cucumber strands, olive oil, vinegar, and finely chopped basil.

5 | Pour 3 tablespoons strawberry juice into each bowl, arrange a few coiled spaghetti strips in the center, and garnish with chopped olives.

Recommended wine: Corbières Rosé 2000, Les Garrigues, Château des Auzines.

Cucumber soup, langoustine sashimi, and pistachio oil

1 | Peel and deseed the cucumbers. Process them in a food processor with the coconut milk. Season with salt and pepper.

2 | Shell the langoustines, sprinkle them with lemon juice, and cut them in half, being careful to remove the black vein along their back.

3 | Serve the cucumber soup in soup plates. Arrange half a langoustine on each side, sprinkle with pistachio oil, and decorate with a strand of fennel.

Recommended wine: Muscadet 2000, Château de la Fessardière (A. Sauvion).

Serves 4

2 cucumbers
7 fl oz (200 ml) unsweetened
    coconut milk
Salt and pepper
4 langoustines
Juice of 1 lemon
Pistachio oil
4 fennel fronds

CUCUMBER
derives from the ancient
Provençal *cogombre*. It is the
fruit of an annual plant of the
Cucurbitaceae (the squash
family). It has long, climbing
stems and the fruit contains
many seeds. Cucumber seeds
have been found in southern
Asia that are estimated to be ten
thousand years old. They were
brought by sailors to the Far
East, Central Asia, and India.
Cucumbers are mentioned
several times in the Bible. The
cucumber's cool, watery flesh
is refreshing, and was one of
the early crops cultivated by
the Children of Israel when they
eventually reached the Holy Land
after wandering in the desert for
forty years. King Louis XIV of
France liked cucumbers very
much; his agronomist, Jean de La
Quintinie, invented greenhouses
in which to grow them so that
the king could enjoy them over
a longer season. Thanks to its
potassium, vitamin C, and folic
acid content, the cucumber is a
powerful diuretic.

Spring roll of cucumber and fresh goat's cheese

1 | Drain the goat's cheese and mix it with the chopped chives and olive oil. Season with salt and pepper.

2 | Shred the cucumber flesh (outside the center of the cucumber) into 20 ribbons around ⅛ inch (3 mm) thick.

3 | Arrange the ribbons on plastic wrap, overlapping each other by ¼ inch (5 mm). Lay horizontally, 1 inch (3 cm) from the bottom on the ribbons, a piece of fresh goat's cheese. Use the plastic wrap to wrap the ribbons around the goat's cheese to form a roll.

4 | Place the roll in the center of the plate and sprinkle a trail of chopped pistachio nuts on one side, crossing it with a chive. Just before serving, brush the cucumber roll with oil.

Recommended wine: Touraine AOC 2003, le Clos du Tue-Bœuf (Puzelat Frères).

Serves 4

1 fresh goat's cheese
2 tablespoons chopped chives
2 tablespoons olive oil
Salt and pepper
2 cucumbers
2 tablespoons chopped
   pistachio nuts
Four whole chives

Zucchini

Green and yellow
zucchini linguini,
with a tomato sauce

1 | Skin and deseed the tomatoes. Process them in a blender with the dried tomatoes and 1 tablespoon olive oil. Set aside.

2 | Use a mandoline to slice the zucchini into ribbons. Set aside.

3 | Dice the bell peppers into ¼-inch (5-mm) pieces. Set aside.

4 | Cover the bottom of a plate with the tomato sauce. Arrange the ribbons of zucchini over the top. Sprinkle with the pieces of bell pepper, sage flowers, chopped fennel fronds, and the Greek and purple basil. Sprinkle with a little olive oil and a few drops of white balsamic vinegar. Serve immediately.

Recommended wine:
Côtes-de-Provence Rosé 2000, Domaine des Fouques.

Serves 4

3 ripe tomatoes
4 sun-dried tomatoes
Extra-virgin olive oil
2 green zucchini
2 yellow zucchini
½ black bell pepper
½ red bell pepper
½ yellow pepper
Sage flowers
Fennel fronds, chopped
Basil, chopped
Purple basil, chopped
White balsamic vinegar

ZUCCHINI are the immature fruit of a type of squash. Squash takes a variety of forms, but zucchini (the word is a diminutive of the Italian *zucca*, a gourd) are eaten before they are fully grown. Squash is a cultivated annual of the Cucurbitaceae family (melon, watermelon, cucumber, etc.) that originated in central America. It is one of the foods that was eaten by native central Americans in pre-Columbian times; it had been cultivated for two thousand years before the Spaniards brought it back to Europe. It acclimatized easily, thanks to its very swift growing cycle. Since it consists of 95 percent water, it is low in calories, but is rich in potassium and vitamin A and also contains vitamin C, folic acid, and copper.

Zucchini spaghetti and pear sandwich with dried tuna flakes

Serves 4

4 zucchini
3 pears
Salt
1 tablespoon white
  balsamic vinegar
1 tablespoon soy sauce
2 tablespoons extra-virgin
  olive oil
1 tablespoon chopped
  oregano
Pepper
Dried tuna flakes
Sage flowers
Oregano leaves

1 | Using a mandoline with fine blades, slice the zucchini into spaghettini-like strands. Refrigerate until required.

2 | Using the flat blade of the mandoline, slice 2 of the pears into 12 slices around 1⁄16 inch (2 mm) thick. Peel and cut the third pear into 1⁄4-inch (5-mm) cubes.

3 | Dissolve a pinch of salt in the white balsamic vinegar. To make the dressing, combine the soy sauce, olive oil, white vinegar, and oregano. Season with pepper.

4 | On a plate rinsed under cold running water, place a small mound of zucchini on a slice of pear and top with a second slice of pear. Do the same for the other plates. Sprinkle with cubes of pear, flakes of tuna, sage flowers, and a few oregano leaves. Finish with a trail of dressing and soy sauce.

Recommended wine:
Saumur Blanc AOC 2000,
Château
Yvonne (Parnay).

Serves 4

7 fl oz (200 ml) whipping cream
¾ oz (20 g) confectioner's sugar
1 mango
Zest and juice of 1 lime
Juice of 2 passion fruit
4 zucchini blossoms
1 tablespoon diced candied
  orange peel

Zucchini blossoms, whipped candied orange cream, and mango and passion-fruit juice

1 | Whip the cream, gradually incorporating the confectioner's sugar, until stiff.

2 | Purée the mango in a blender. Add a few drops of lime juice and the passion-fruit juice. Refrigerate until required.

3 | Use a piping bag to stuff the zucchini blossoms with the whipped cream mixture. Sprinkle with the diced candied orange peel and the lime zest. Pour a trail of mango-passion sauce around the blossoms. Serve immediately.

Recommended wine: Vouvray Moelleux AOC 2002, La Ferme (Lemaire-Fournier).

Serves 4

2 fennel bulbs
2 limes
9 oz (250 g) salmon fillet
Extra-virgin olive oil
Pepper
4 sprigs dill
2 teaspoons grated
   ginger root

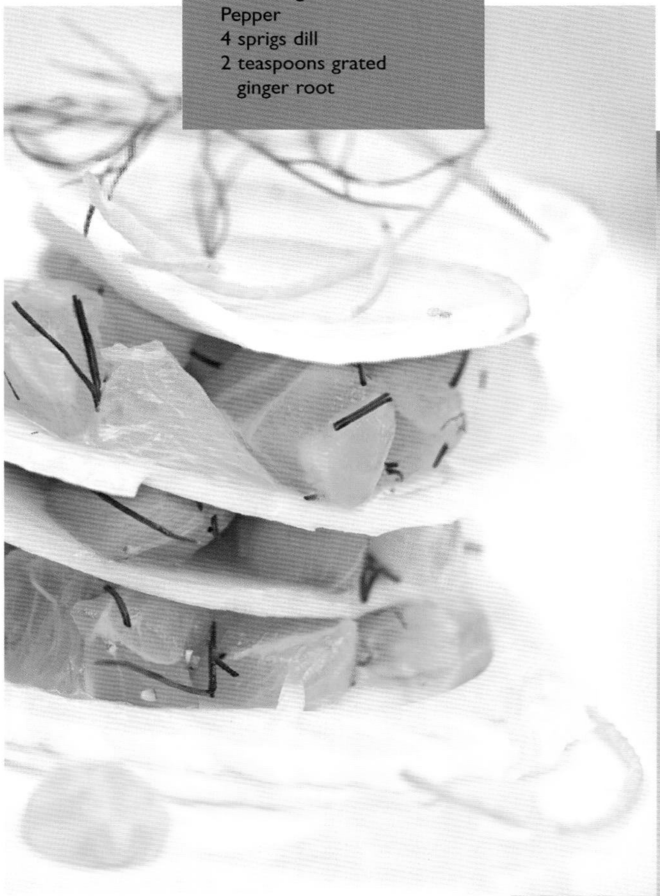

Fennel, salmon, and lime millefeuille

1 | Use a mandoline to slice the fennel bulbs into 16 slices ⅛ inch (3 mm) thick.

2 | Peel the limes, discarding the pith. Cut each segment into three pieces.

3 | Dice the salmon into ¼-inch (5-mm) cubes. Place in a salad bowl. Chop 1 sprig of dill. Mix it with the salmon and add a sprinkling of olive oil. Sprinkle with pepper.

4 | On a plate, arrange 1 slice of fennel; cover with salmon cubes and a few pieces of lime. Do this twice more. End with a sprig of dill, accompanied by a half a teaspoonful of grated ginger. Sprinkle with a little olive oil. Serve immediately.

Recommended wine: White Vin de Pays de Vaucluse 1999, Château La Canorgue.

Fennel

Cream of fennel, brocciù cheese, avocado, and fennel seeds

1 | Peel and pit the avocados, and cut them into ¼-inch (5-mm) cubes. Sprinkle with lemon juice and set aside.

2 | In a blender, mix the fennel bulbs with water, a little olive oil, salt and pepper. Set aside.

3 | Mash the brocciù cheese with a fork, sprinkle it with a little olive oil and set aside.

4 | Place a little brocciù in the middle of a soup plate. Pour the fennel cream around it. Cover the cheese with a few avocado cubes. Sprinkle with the seeded fennel flowers, then with a little olive oil. Serve immediately.

Recommended wine: White Côtes-de-Provence 1999, Grande Cuvée Delphine, Domaine Saint-André-de-Figuière.

Serves 4

2 avocados
Juice of 1 lemon
2 fennel bulbs
13 fl oz (375 ml) water
Extra-virgin olive oil
Salt and pepper
4 oz (120 g) brocciù cheese
Seeded fennel flowers

FENNEL derives from the classic Latin *faeniculum*, which is a diminutive of the word *faenum*, meaning "hay." Fennel is a perennial of the Umbelliferae family, which includes dill, parsley, carrot, celery, and parsnip, and originated in the Mediterreanean. It was cultivated in antiquity by the Greeks and Romans, who enjoyed it as a vegetable as well as for its medicinal properties. Raw fennel is an excellent source of potassium. It contains vitamin C, folic acid, magnesium, calcium, and phosphorus. It is also a diuretic, antispasmodic, and stimulant, and helps relieve gastric pain and clean out the digestive system.

Fennel carpaccio
with orange, passion fruit, and sage flowers

1 | Peel the 4 oranges, discarding all the pith. Slice them into rounds.

2 | Using a mandoline, slice the fennel into rings about ¹⁄₁₆ inch (2 mm) thick.

3 | Scoop the inside of the passion fruit into a bowl.

4 | Finely chop the bird's-eye chili pepper.

5 | On a plate rinsed in cold water, arrange three rounds of orange. Cover with rings of fennel and sprinkle with a few chopped fennel leaves, sage flowers, and the chopped chili pepper. Sprinkle everything generously with olive oil. Garnish with 1 teaspoon passion fruit juice and seeds.

Recommended wine: White Bergerac Sec 1998, Cuvée Sophie, Grande Maison.

Serves 4

4 oranges
2 fennel bulbs
2 passion fruit
1 bird's-eye chili pepper
Fennel fronds, chopped
20 sage flowers
Extra-virgin olive oil
Salt and pepper

Fig

FIG, from the vulgar Latin *fica*. The edible fruit of the fig tree, formed from the entire inflorescence, which becomes fleshy after fertilization. There are more than 150 varieties of fig tree. The fig originated in the Near East and has been highly prized since antiquity for its nutritional and medicinal properties. The Greeks and Romans were particularly enamored of the fig and they brought it to Europe. The Spanish also loved figs and took them along on their missionary conquests of the New World. Long before sugar was easily obtainable, figs were used to sweeten foods. The high fiber content of the fig makes it a powerful laxative and diuretic. It also contains a considerable amount of mineral salts and vitamins.

Figs with fig-and-yogurt jelly

1 | In a food processor combine the 8 fresh figs, 1 dried fig, and muscovado sugar. Fill the glasses two-thirds full of the mixture. Set them aside.

2 | Soak the gelatin leaves in water for 10 minutes to soften them.

3 | Put the yogurt, sugar, and gelatin leaves into a bowl. Beat with a whisk.

4 | Fill the last third of the glasses with this yogurt jelly. Decorate with a sprig of white currants and a small piece of dried fig.

Recommended wine: Muscat de Rivesaltes 2001, Domaine de Blanes (M.-P. Bories)

Serves 4

8 fresh figs
2 dried figs
4 teaspoons muscovado sugar
5 gelatine leaves
4 pots of live yogurt
4 teaspoons sugar
4 sprigs of white currants

Serves 4

7 oz (200 g) fresh goat's
   cheese
2 tablespoons chopped
   pistachios
2 tablespoons lavender
   honey
Pepper
8 fresh figs
4 fresh lavender flowers

Fig, sikinos-style

1 | In a bowl, mash the fresh goat's
cheese with the chopped
pistachios, and 1 tablespoon
lavender honey. Season with
pepper.

2 | Slice the figs into 16 slices
¼ inch (5 mm) thick.

3 | Place a slice of fig in the bottom
of each plate. Cover with 1
teaspoon of the goat's cheese
mixture. Do this twice more.
Finish with 1 chopped pistachio.
Surround with a trail of honey
and garnish with 1 lavender
flower.

Recommended wine:
Vinsanto 1998.

Fig, brocciù cheese, and maple syrup

1 | Mash the brocciù with a fork, and add 2 teaspoons of maple syrup and 1 pinch Szechuan pepper. Mix well and keep in the refrigerator.

2 | Cut a cross in the figs and open them by two-thirds. Stuff them with the brocciù mixture. Cover with a seeded fennel flower. Sprinkle with a little maple syrup.

Recommended wine: Muscat 2000, Mas Amiel.

Serves 4

8 oz (250 g) brocciù cheese
Maple syrup
Szechuan pepper
8 figs
8 seeded fennel flowers

Foie gras

Fig and foie gras
morsels

Serves 4

8 dried figs
1 foie gras
Balsamic vinegar
Salt and pepper
4 dried rhubarb stems

1 | Slice the dried figs in half crosswise.

2 | Place half a fig on a plate. Cover with
a shaving of foie gras and sprinkle
with a drop of balsamic vinegar.
Season with salt and pepper.
Arrange a piece of dried rhubarb
stem on one side.

Recommended wine:
Gewürztraminer, Late Harvest 1997,
Grand Cru Streinert (Pierre Frick).

FOIE GRAS, from the vulgar Latin *ficatum* which
meant liver from a goose fattened on figs. By
carefully observing nature, the ancient Egyptians
noticed that wild geese "prepared" for their
migrations by gorging themselves, thus storing
energy in the form of fat in the liver. This gave the
Egyptians the idea of gorging the geese so as to
enable them to eat this hypertrophied liver. The
Greeks and Romans did the same. The former fed
the geese a mixture of wheat and water, the latter
figs. Today, corn, lard, beans, and salt are the
mixture with which the geese are force-fed. Foie
gras is high in fat [44 percent per 3½ oz (100 g)].
Although the practice of force-feeding geese and
ducks has been condemned by some animal
activists in the West, there is no evidence
that the creatures find it unpleasant.

Serves 4

1 duck foie gras
1 orange carrot
1 yellow carrot
1 cauliflower
2 asparagus stems
1 beet
1 Jerusalem artichoke
1 green apple
8 Chinese chives
Sea salt
Freshly ground pepper

Foie gras carpaccio, roots, and fall fruit

1 | Freeze the foie gras for 30 minutes.

2 | Using a mandoline, slice all the vegetables and fruit into ¼-inch (2-mm) strips.

3 | Run a very sharp knife blade under warm running water. Cut 4 slices of ¼-inch (4-mm) thick foie gras, lengthwise.

4 | On a large chilled serving platter, arrange all the ingredients elegantly, finishing with 2 Chinese chives. Season with salt and pepper. Serve immediately.

Recommended wine: Vouvray Moelleux 1998, Premier Cru de Tris (Huet).

Serves 4

1 foie gras
28 spears wild asparagus
Aged balsamic vinegar
Freshly ground pepper
Sea salt

Foie gras and wild asparagus with balsamic vinegar

1 | Freeze the foie gras for 30 minutes.

2 | Cut the tips from 20 of the asparagus spears.

3 | Cut 4 slices of foie gras around ½ inch (1 cm) thick.

4 | On each chilled plate, arrange 1 slice of foie gras and top it with 5 wild asparagus tips. On one side, trail a little aged balsamic vinegar and sprinkle with a pinch of coarsely ground pepper. Season the foie gras with a pinch of sea salt. Decorate the side of each plate with two crossed asparagus spears.

Recommended wine: 15-Year-Old Maury.

Serves 4

Prepare the day before serving
9 oz (250 g) strawberries
1 small cucumber
1 red bell pepper
2 tomatoes
1 slice white bread
Extra-virgin olive oil
Sherry vinegar
Coarse salt
Espelette chili pepper
1 celery stalk

Tomato and strawberry gazpacho

1 | The night before, wash and dice all the ingredients except the celery. Process all the ingredients except the celery in a food processor. Strain through a conical sieve and set aside in the refrigerator in a large bowl.

2 | On the day itself, pour the gazpacho into a tall glass and add a celery stick.

Recommended wine: Tourmaline Rosé 2000, Château de Peyrassol-Plassous (Mme Rigord).

STRAWBERRY: the name derives from the habit of raising cultivated strawberries on beds of straw. Strictly speaking, strawberries are not fruit. The flesh that we eat is the result of an inflation of the stem, which is produced after pollination. The tiny yellow seeds on the outside of the fruit are the actual fruit itself. The strawberry bush grows in all the temperate parts of the world. Some varieties yield more than one crop a year. In 1714, the Frenchman François Amédé Frézier crossed two varieties of wild strawberry, producing a large, fat strawberry that was widely cultivated in Europe. This is the ancestor, after many crosses and hybrids, of the strawberry we eat today. There are currently over 600 varieties of strawberries. The strawberry is rich in vitamins B_x and C, potassium, folic acid, and magnesium. It is reputed to have diuretic, purgative, and astringent properties.

Strawberry, pineapple, and tomato minestrone

1 | Wash and deseed the tomatoes. Process them in a food processor with the white balsamic vinegar and a pinch of salt. Strain them through a conical sieve and refrigerate until required.

2 | Peel the pineapple and cut it into ½-inch (1-cm) cubes.

3 | Quickly wash the strawberries, hull them, and cut them into ½-inch (1-cm) cubes.

4 | Cover the bottom of a soup plate with the tomato. Arrange an equal quantity of pineapple and strawberries over the top. Sprinkle with the fennel fronds and then with a little olive oil. Serve immediately.

Recommended wine:
Minervois Late Harvest 1996, Domaine de La-Tour-Boisée.

Serves 4

4 tomatoes
2 teaspoons white
    balsamic vinegar
Salt
1 pineapple
12 strawberries
Fennel fronds
Extra-virgin olive oil

Strawberries
in disguise

1 | Quickly wash the strawberries without hulling them and arrange them on absorbent paper.

2 | Fill a small cup with balsamic vinegar. Dip a strawberry in it to two-thirds of its length. Sprinkle with grated parmesan. Repeat, and line up 3 strawberries on each plate.

Recommended wine: Vin Cuit de Provence, Domaine des Bastides.

Serves 4

12 strawberries
Balsamic vinegar (at least 10 years old)
9 oz (250 g) grated parmesan cheese

Raspberry, lychee, and rose-petal frozen yogurt

1 | The night before serving, pour the yogurt, lychees, rose water, and sugar into a large bowl, and mix them gently using a spatula.

2 | Using plastic wrap, cover a serving platter large enough to hold 4 hoops measuring 4 inches (10 cm). Place the hoops on the platter and arrange 3 raspberries in the bottom of the circle and 5 around the walls. Carefully pour in the yogurt mixture until the circles are half-full. Add a few more raspberries and fill to the top with yogurt. Freeze until required.

3 | On the day itself, serve these parfaits at the start of the meal, unmolding them by holding a thin blade under hot water then running it around the inside of the molds. Garnish with a rose petal.

Recommended wine: Beaumes-de-Venise, Domaine de Durban.

Serves 4

Prepare the night before serving
4 pots of thick yogurt
16 lychees
1 tablespoon rose water
⅓ cup granulated sugar
24 raspberries
4 rose petals

Raspberry, fig, and banana "tartlets"

Serves 4

2 bananas
Juice and zest of 1 lime
¾ tablespoon sugar
4 figs
2 dried bananas
12 raspberries
8 chopped pistachios
Thyme or rosemary honey

1 | Peel the bananas and sprinkle them with lime zest. Mash the bananas with a fork, adding the lime juice and the sugar. Set the purée aside.

2 | Cut the figs into pieces that are the same size as the raspberries. Set aside.

3 | Roll up the dried banana slices around a ring 4 inches (10 cm) in diameter.

4 | Carefully transfer the banana ring to a plate. Garnish the bottom of the plate with 1 tablespoon banana purée. Inside arrange, alternately, 1 piece of fig and 1 raspberry. End with a few pieces of pistachio and a few drops of thyme or rosemary honey.

Recommended wine: Vouvray Late Harvest 1989, Cuvée Constance (Huet).

Raspberry

RASPBERRY, from the Frankish *brambasi* meaning "berry of the brambles." The delicate white flowers of the raspberry produce the fruit, which actually consist of a number of tiny seeds in a cluster. The wild raspberry (smaller than its domesticated cousin) is of prehistoric origin and has left traces in eastern Asia. The first cultivated variety was discovered in Turkey by the Crusaders and was known as *Rubus idaeus*, named after the Ida mountain chain in Asia Minor. It was not until the nineteenth century that the raspberry was generally adopted in Europe and North America. The raspberry contains vitamins A and C, potassium and magnesium, and has a high fiber content. It gives good results when used to combat heartburn and constipation. The raspberry, a climbing plant, puts out shoots in spring that, when peeled, are delicious eaten raw.

Serves 4

40 raspberries
10 peeled and boned
   sardine fillets
Aged balsamic vinegar
1 small box white
   currants

Raspberry and
sardine morsels
in balsamic vinegar

Wrap each of 10 raspberries in half a sardine fillet and arrange them
on a plate. Sprinkle the plate with a few drops of aged balsamic vinegar
and scatter the whitecurrants around the raspberries.

Recommended wine: Corbières Rosé 2000, Château des Auzines.

PASSION FRUIT, also known as granadilla. This excellent fruit originated in Brazil and has a flavor that is reminiscent of the pomegranate (granadilla is a diminutive of the Spanish word for pomegranate, *granada*). When describing the flower in 1737, Linnaeus gave it the name of *flos passionis*. Much later, in the mid-twentieth century, once this exotic fruit had found its way to Europe, the name "passion fruit" came to be used in English. Of the four hundred species found in the wild, only thirty produce edible fruit. The number of varieties sold commercially is even smaller. Passion fruit is an excellent source of vitamins A and C, potassium, sodium, iron, magnesium, and phosphorus, and is known for its anti-spasmodic properties. The seeds are used as a vermifuge.

Raspberries in a mango sandwich with passion-fruit juice

1 | Whip the cream. Fold in the vanilla sugar. Refrigerate until required. Chill the plates.

2 | Peel the mangoes and cut them into ¼-inch (5-mm) thick slices. Cut out 8 rectangles using a rectangular cookie cutter measuring 3 x 1½ inches (7.5 x 3.5 cm).

3 | On each chilled plate, arrange 1 rectangle of mango, 8 raspberries, and 1 scoop of whipped cream. Sprinkle with a few drops of lavender honey. Cover with a second rectangle of mango. End with a trail of passion fruit around the sandwich.

Recommended wine: Baumes-de-Venise.

Serves 4

⅔ cup (150 ml) whipping cream
1 pack vanilla sugar
2 mangoes
32 raspberries
Lavender honey
2 passion fruit

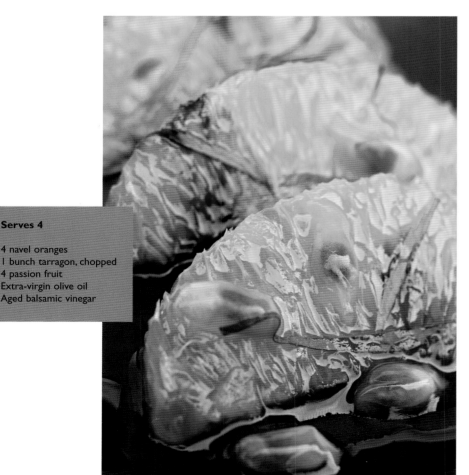

Serves 4

4 navel oranges
1 bunch tarragon, chopped
4 passion fruit
Extra-virgin olive oil
Aged balsamic vinegar

Orange, passion fruit, and tarragon carpaccio

Peel the orange, discarding the pith. Arrange the segments on each plate. Sprinkle with the tarragon leaves. Pour a tablespoon of passion fruit pulp over the orange. Add a sprinkle of olive oil and one of aged balsamic vinegar.

Recommended wine: Sélection de Grains Nobles 2001, Alsace.

Serves 4

8 small passion fruit
1 red chili pepper
8 shiso leaves
4 oz (125 g) salmon
Zest of 1 lime
Sea salt
4 scallops
Chive flowers

Scallop passion, salmon passion

1 | Cut the passion fruit in half and scoop out the flesh, setting it aside in a bowl. Wash and dry the passion-fruit skins and set them aside for assembling the dish.

2 | Chop the chili pepper and finely chop the shiso leaves.

3 | Dice the salmon and scallops into ¼-inch (5-mm) cubes. Place in two separate bowls. Sprinkle each with the lime zest, chopped chili pepper, and chopped shiso. Add 1 tablespoon passion fruit to each of the bowls. Fold together. Season with salt.

4 | Fill half the passion fruit shells with the salmon tartare and the other half with the scallops. Arrange one shell of each on each plate. Garnish with a few chive flowers.

Recommended wine: Condrieu 1999, Domaine A.-Perret.

Oyster

OYSTER, from the Latin *ostrea* and the Greek *ostreon*. Consumption of oysters dates back to prehistory. It was particularly popular with the Romans, the Celts, and the Greeks. In Ancient Greece, oysters were both eaten and used as ballot papers. The electors used to scratch their vote on an oyster shell. Since it is not hard to rear this marine bivalve, oyster farming has been practiced for over two thousand years. The first peoples to do so intensively were the Romans and the Gauls.

There are two types of oyster, the flat and the rounded, both of which are graded by numbers which decrease with size: the smaller the number, the bigger and fatter the oyster.

When choosing oysters, make sure they are tightly closed and heavy; otherwise it may be that they have lost their liquid. They can be kept in seaweed-filled baskets for a week, on condition that they are kept as cool as on the bottom shelf of the refrigerator. The temperature should be around 41–59°F (5–15°C). Oysters should be tightly packed and protected by a lid with a weight on it, to prevent them from opening up and losing their liquid.

Oysters are rich in vitamin B_{12}, iron, zinc, and copper, and are said to be nourishing and have regenerative properties.

Oyster and blood-orange jelly

Serves 4

3 gelatin leaves
6 blood oranges
12 oysters
6 arugula flowers
  or 6 borage flowers

1 | Begin by soaking the gelatin leaves in a bowl of iced water.

2 | Squeeze the oranges. Warm the juice obtained in a saucepan, reduce it by one-third, and skim off any impurities that rise to the surface.

3 | Drain the gelatin leaves. Add them to the reduced orange juice, and mix quickly. Cover a cake pan with plastic wrap and pour the mixture into the pan. Refrigerate until the jelly has set.

4 | Open the oysters: they should give up their liquid. Set them aside on ice.

5 | Cut the jello into ½-inch (10-mm) cubes. Arrange 2 or 3 cubes of blood-orange jelly on each oyster, accompanied by 1 arugula flower (for its spicy touch) or borage (for its iodine odor).

Recommended wine: Savennières Coulée-de-Serrant Blanc 1999, Château de La-Roche-aux-Moines.

Oyster with puréed cucumber, caviar, and kumquat

1 | Peel and deseed the cucumber. Blend in a food processor with the light cream. Season with salt and pepper. Refrigerate until required.

2 | Open the oysters. Pull off their beards.

3 | Pour 1 tablespoon of cream of cucumber into a soup plate. Place 1 oyster on top. Finish with a small scoop of caviar and 2 kumquat zests. Sprinkle with a few dill leaves.

Recommended wine: Champagne Sec Ansaltme Saltosse.

Serves 4

1 cucumber
3 tablespoons light cream
Salt and white pepper
4 G2 or Pacific oysters
1 teaspoon caviar
Zest of 8 kumquats
Dill

Oyster, blood-orange, and lime seviche

1 | Open the oysters. Save their liquid. Remove them from their shells and set them aside in a large bowl placed on ice.

2 | Using a mandoline, slice the red onion into thin rounds. Then use the fine blade to slice half a cucumber into long, spaghetti-like strands.

3 | Finely chop the 2 chili-pepper halves.

4 | Peel 2 blood oranges, discarding the pith. Separate the segments, then cut them into 2 or 3 sections. Squeeze the other 2 blood oranges and 3 limes.

5 | Arrange the fruit and juice in the bowl containing the oysters. Season with sea salt.

6 | Place 4 glasses on ice. Arrange 3 oysters in each glass. Sprinkle with lime juice and 4 coriander leaves. Serve immediately.

Recommended wine: Pouilly Fumé 2002, Pur Sang (Didier Dagueneau).

Serves 4

12 oysters (preferably
  "prat ar coum")
1 red onion
½ cucumber
½ small yellow chili pepper
½ small red chili pepper
4 blood oranges
4 limes
16 coriander leaves,
  coarsely chopped
Sea salt

Langoustine cup
with purple potatoes

Serves 4

16 average-size
  langoustines
2 purple potatoes
½ melon
8–10 strawberries
2 cups (500 ml) rice
  vinegar
1 teaspoon soy sauce
Lemon juice
Superfine sugar
Mixed herbs
Salt

1 | Shell the langoustines and season them with rice vinegar, soy sauce, and a pinch of sugar and salt.

2 | Peel the purple potatoes and slice them into rounds ⅛ inch (1 mm) thick. Sprinkle lightly with salt and lemon juice.

3 | Do the same with the strawberries. Finely dice half the melon.

4 | In a sundae glass, arrange a layer of fruit, and line the sides with the potato rounds. Add a little of the langoustine preparation, then garnish with the chopped herbs.

Recommended wine:
Meursault Premier Cru 1999, Les Charmes (Vincent Girardin).

Vegetable
brunoise

1 | For the yellow carrot sauce: blend the yellow carrot in a food processor. Add the soy milk, lemon juice, 1 tablespoon olive oil, and 1 pinch of salt to the carrot juice.

2 | For the brunoise: finely dice the vegetables. Season them with salt and orange juice.

3 | Shell the langoustines and season them with a pinch of salt and a little olive oil.

4 | Place a small hoop in the middle of a plate. Arrange a layer of the vegetable brunoise inside it, then add a layer of the langoustine. Garnish the dish with herbs and thyme flowers. Trace a thin line of carrot sauce around the dish.

Recommended wine: Pouilly Fumé Blanc 2000, Cuvée Silex (Didier Dagueneau).

goustine

LANGOUSTINE is a dimunitive of *langouste*, or lobster, which in turn derives from the vulgar Latin *lacusta*, from the classic Latin *locusta* meaning "grasshopper." The langoustine is also known as the Dublin Bay Prawn or Norway lobster. It has the size and shape of a large crawfish, but it lives in salt water on the European side of the Atlantic and in the Mediterranean. The langoustine is rich in calcium, phosphorus, and iron. If langoustines are not available, substitute jumbo shrimps, crayfish, or crawfish.

Serves 4

2 white asparagus
16 medium langoustines
2 shiso leaves
Zest of 1 orange
  or 1 kumquat
Salt
Lemon juice
Vanilla extract
Cardamom extract
Olive oil
Thyme or borage flowers
Arugula

Langoustine tartare with strips of white asparagus

1 | Cut the asparagus into thin strips 2¾–3¼ inches (7–8 cm) long and ¹⁄₁₆ in (2 mm) thick.

2 | Shell the langoustines and cut them into small pieces. Season them with the chopped shiso leaves, the orange or kumquat zest, a pinch of salt, a little lemon juice, and a drop each of vanilla extract and cardamom extract.

3 | On each plate, arrange the langoustine preparation by "wedging" it between strips of asparagus. Sprinkle with a little olive oil. Garnish with the rest of the orange zest and with thyme or borage flowers and sprigs of arugula.

Recommended wine: Riesling Grand Cru 2000, Kastelberg, Domaine Kreydenweiss.

Mango

MANGO, from the Portuguese *manga*, itself derived from the Tamil *man-kay*, referring to the fleshy edible fruit ("*kay*") of the mango tree. The mango, which originated in India, has a large pit that clings to the flesh. It has been cultivated for over six thousand years. The mango nevertheless remained unknown outside Asia for a long time. It was introduced to Brazil by Portuguese explorers in the eighteenth century, and from there it gradually spread around the world. It is related to the pistachio tree and the cashew tree and only grows in the tropics. There are over a thousand varieties of mangoes; they may vary from a spherical to a more oval shape. The mango is very rich in vitamins A and C, potassium, and copper.

Mango, avocado, pear, and carrot maki

1 | Combine the rice vinegar, white balsamic vinegar, maple syrup, and soy sauce.

2 | Trim the mango, carrot, avocados, and pear into matchstick strips at least ⅜ inch (8 mm) long. Sprinkle them with lemon juice.

3 | Slice 1 sheet of nori vertically. Make a bundle consisting of 1 mango strip, 1 carrot strip, 1 avocado strip, 1 pear strip, and 1 chive. Roll each bundle in a piece of nori. Arrange 3 of these bundles, or maki, on each plate, accompanied by a little ring of sauce.

Recommended wine: Bugey Blanc 2003.

Mango and duck millefeuille

1 | Dissolve a pinch of salt in the mango vinegar. Process in a food processor with the hazelnut oil. Season with pepper.

2 | Peel the mangoes. Purée half a mango and slice the rest into strips ⅛ inch (3 mm) thick.

3 | Arrange a millefeuille consisting of alternating slices of mango, duck, spinach leaves, and daikon sprouts, ending with spinach and daikon. Sprinkle with the dressing. Scatter white and redcurrants around the sandwich and finish with a few trails of mango purée.

Recommended wine: Banyuls.

Serves 4

8 beet tops
20 basil leaves
2 green apples
Juice of 1 lime
3 mangoes
Pimento paste
Extra-virgin olive oil

Mango and green apple salad

1 | Cut the beet tops into pieces ⅝ inch (15 mm) long.

2 | Finely chop the basil.

3 | Wash the green apples but do not peel them. Use a mandoline to cut them into slices ¹⁄₁₆–⅛ inch (2–3 mm) thick. Sprinkle with lime juice and refrigerate until required.

4 | Peel the mangoes and cut them into ¼-inch (4-mm) slices.

5 | Arrange a few mango slices on a plate. Cover with the apple rounds. Sprinkle with chopped basil. Throw a few matchstick strips of beet tops over them. Surround with pimento paste and sprinkle with a little olive oil.

Recommended wine: Muscat d'Alsace 2001.

Mackerel seviche

Serves 4

4 mackerel fillets, skinned and boned
1 red onion
½ yellow bell pepper
½ red bell pepper
2 limes
20 matchstick strips of ginger root
Juice of 1 orange
1 tablespoon chopped fresh coriander
16 gooseberries
20 white currants
1 teaspoon pimento paste
Sea salt
16 fresh coriander leaves for the garnish

1 | Two hours before serving, place 4 small bowls into 4 larger bowls filled with crushed ice and place them in the freezer.

2 | Use a mandoline to slice the red onion, yellow bell pepper and red bell pepper into thin strips. Then dice the strips of pepper into ¼-inch (5-mm) cubes. Set aside in a cool place.

3 | Peel 1 lime, removing the pith, separate the segments and cut them into 3. Refrigerate.

4 | Slice the mackerel fillets into ½-inch (1-cm) cubes.

5 | In a salad bowl, combine all the ingredients with the zest of the second lime and sprinkle with salt.

6 | Distribute the seviche between the 4 bowls on ice. Sprinkle with 4 coriander leaves per bowl.

Recommended wine: Ménetou-Salon 2002, Château de Maupas.

Mackerel and grapefruit
with pesto sauce

1 | Peel the pomelos, discarding the pith, and separate the segments. Keep them chilled.

2 | In a mortar, crush the basil leaves, sea salt, and pepper. Sprinkle with olive oil and mix well.

3 | Slice the mackerel into pieces ½ inch (1 cm) thick.

4 | On each chilled plate, press segments of grapefruit up to the slices of mackerel. Sprinkle with the pesto. Serve immediately.

Recommended wine: Côtes-du-Rhône Viognier 2001, Domaine Gramenon.

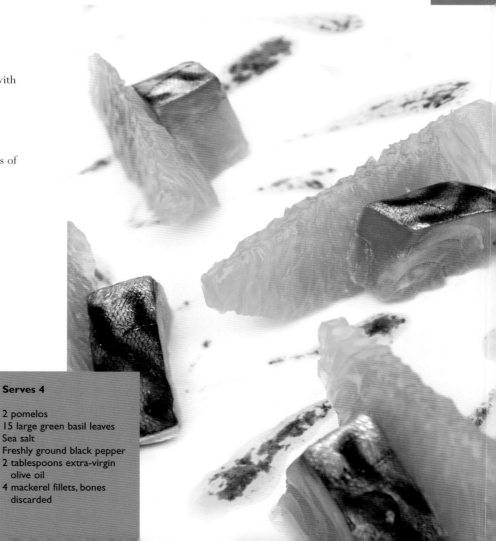

Serves 4

2 pomelos
15 large green basil leaves
Sea salt
Freshly ground black pepper
2 tablespoons extra-virgin olive oil
4 mackerel fillets, bones discarded

Mackerel

MACKEREL, from Middle German *makelâre*, meaning "broker," from *makeln*, "dealing."
This fish of the temperate seas has acquired a bad reputation in parts of Europe: it is supposed
to act as a broker in bringing female herrings to male herrings during their long migrations.
Its French name, *maquereau*, is therefore also used to mean "a pimp." The etymology of the name
is the same as "smack," meaning "to beat or hit," to cover with marks. The mackerel is, in other
words, a fish covered with blue-green markings. It lives in large shoals that migrate out to sea
in winter. Varieties of mackerel are found from Morocco to the White Sea, and from the
Mediterranean to the Black Sea. It is also plentiful in the Atlantic and Pacific oceans.
The mackerel, being an oily fish and a relative of the tuna, is particularly rich in omega 3,
which has a beneficial effect on the cardiovascular system.

Serves 4

1 red onion
White balsamic vinegar
16 slices cured duck
 (see recipe page 64)
4 mackerel fillets, boned
1 bunch borage
 flowers

Mackerel, duck, and borage flower, sashimi-style

1 | Two hours before serving, use the mandoline to slice the red onion and marinate it in white balsamic vinegar.

2 | Cut two matchstick strips of cured duck from each slice.

3 | Dice the mackerel fillets into ½-inch (1-cm) cubes.

4 | Rinse a plate under cold water and arrange a few pieces of mackerel on it. Cross on top of it 1 marinated onion ring and 1 strip of cured duck. Add a borage flower. Serve immediately.

Recommended wine: White Coteaux-d'Aix-en-Provence 2002.

Melon

MELON, from the low Latin *melo, -onis*, and classical Latin *melopepo*, itself derived from the Greek *melopepon* from *melon* (apple) and *pepon* (gourd). The melon is the fruit of an annual climbing plant of the Cucurbitaceae family that includes cucumber, zucchini, squash, and watermelon. Melons need a lot of sunlight and generous watering and are classified into winter and summer varieties. Winter melons are ovoid in shape and keep for longer. The melon is the only vegetable that originated in the southern part of Africa, but it has come a long way since its distant origins. Thanks to intensive and exhaustive selection, the fruit, which was originally the size of an apple, is now the size of a football. In Egypt in the fourth century it was already a larger, sweeter, and less bitter plant than the original. It then disappeared from history for more than a millennium, re-emerging in fifteenth century France, under King Charles VIII. In 1883, sixty-five varieties were known. The melon consists mainly of water; its nutritional value is contained in the six to eight percent of sugars present in the flesh. The melon is an excellent source of potassium, vitamin C, and folic acid. It is diuretic, laxative, and acts as a stimulus to the appetite.

Melon and tuna maki
with fennel flowers

Serves 4

1 tablespoon soy sauce
1 teaspoon rice vinegar
1 tablespoon honey
1 teaspoon wasabi
2 melons
9 oz (250 g) tuna fillet
1 black radish
12 sheets nori,
   3¾ x 3 in (9 x 5 cm)
12 chives
12 fennel flowers

1 | Combine the soy sauce, rice vinegar, honey and wasabi. Set aside the dressing.

2 | Peel and deseed the melons. Cut them into strips measuring 2 x ¾ inches (5 x 2 cm) wide , and ½ inch (1 cm) long. Proceed in the same way with the tuna.

3 | Cut the black radish into 12 matchstick strips, 2 inches (5 cm) long and ⅛ inch (3 mm) wide.

4 | Cut a sheet of nori lengthwise. In the lower part, place 1 strip of melon, and top it with a piece of tuna, and a piece of black radish surrounded by two chives. Roll the nori round it to make it into a maki sushi. Garnish each with 1 fennel flower. Sprinkle a drop of dressing in front of each maki.

Recommended wine:
White Coteaux-du-Languedoc 2002.

Melon and ginger soup
with sesame seeds

1 | Peel and deseed the melons. Process them in the food processor with the olive oil, grated ginger, and a pinch of salt.

2 | Fill 4 soup bowls with the melon. Top with a few shavings of ginger and a few sesame seeds.

Recommended wine: Muscat de Saint-Jean-de-Minervois 2000, Domaine des Comtés.

Serves 4

2 melons
1 tablespoon extra-virgin
   olive oil
1 teaspoon grated ginger
Sea salt (preferably
   Maldon)
White sesame seeds

Melon mozza

1 | The night before, chop the chili pepper and marinate it in olive oil.

2 | Peel and deseed the melons. Cut them into large slices.

3 | Tear the mozzarella into small pieces.

4 | Arrange a few melon slices and pieces of mozzarella on a plate. Sprinkle with 8 basil leaves. Sprinkle with a little of the peppery olive oil. Season with salt and serve immediately.

Recommended wine: Grammenon 2003 Rosé (M. Aubéry-Clément).

Serves 4

1 fresh chili pepper
2 tablespoons extra-virgin olive oil
2 melons
2 balls of buffalo mozzarella
32 basil leaves
Sea salt

Egg

EGG is from the Anglo-Saxon "eigg." The egg has long been a symbol of fertility among pagans as well as in the monotheistic religions. Certain traditions practiced by the Ancient Egyptians, the Chinese, the Persians, and the Greeks have persisted, such as that of decorating the shells. Easter was associated with eggs in eras when hens rarely laid in winter. With the return of spring, which corresponded with the laying cycle, Easter was celebrated, first as the festival of the goddess Eastre, later as the Christian festival. Furthermore, since the eggs were considered to be a rich food, they were forbidden during Lent—Christians had to wait until Easter in order to be allowed to eat them again. The larger the egg, the more nourishing it is, whatever its origin and color. Egg proteins are said to be complete, because they supply the eight essential amino acids that the human body cannot produce for itself. Eggs also contain vitamins (B_{12} and D), folic acid, phosphorus, zinc, iron, and potassium.

Coconut milk
eggnog

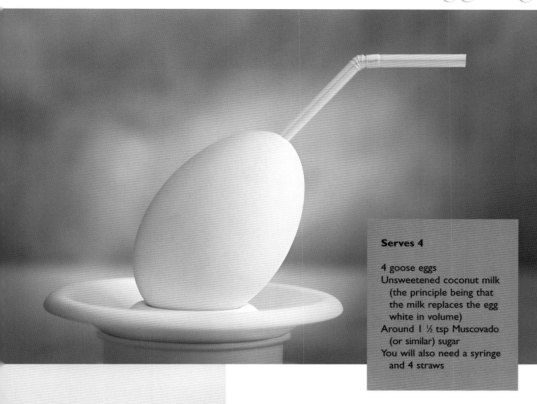

1 | Wash the eggs. Use a needle to gently pierce the base of one egg.

2 | Still working carefully, use the tip of a small vegetable knife to pierce the top of the egg, making a hole the diameter of a straw. Use a syringe to blow out the contents of the egg, emptying them into a bowl separating the white from the yolk.

3 | Mix the egg yolks with the coconut milk and sugar. Use a syringe to fill the eggs with the mixture obtained.

4 | Drink very cold.

The whites can be used to make iced meringues.

Serves 4

4 goose eggs
Unsweetened coconut milk
(the principle being that
the milk replaces the egg
white in volume)
Around 1 ½ tsp Muscovado
(or similar) sugar
You will also need a syringe
and 4 straws

Snow White

1 | Whip the egg whites until stiff, adding the granulated sugar and pepper at the end. Pour them into a small rectangular mold and freeze for 3 hours.

2 | Mix the egg yolks with the Muscovado sugar, marsala, and cream.

3 | Unmold the whites and cut them into even rectangles.

4 | Place a snow white rectangle on each plate. Serve the marsala cream in a tall glass.

Recommended wine: Loupiac.

Serves 4

4 hen's eggs, separated
3½ cups granulated sugar
6 grinds of white pepper
2½ tbsp Muscovado sugar
2 fl oz (60 ml) marsala or
  maple syrup
2 fl oz (60 ml) whipping cream

Faux
carbonara

1 | Cut the slices of coppa into small strips. Mix with the hen's egg
yolk, the cream, and half the lemon juice. Season and set aside.

2 | Using a mandoline fitted with a fine blade, slice the celery root
into spaghetti-like strands. Sprinkle with olive oil, the other half
of the lemon juice, pepper, and salt.

3 | Take the quail eggs and separate the whites from the yolks.

4 | Arrange a mound of celery root spaghetti on each plate. Place the
yolk of a quail's egg inside an eggshell and place this on top of the
celery root. Sprinkle with the coppa mixture.

Recommended wine: Tokay Pinot Gris 1999, Cuvée de l'Ours
(Charles Frey).

Watermelon

WATERMELON is another type of melon, a member of the Cucurbitaceae or squash family, that grows in the tropics. It first came to Europe from the Arab world, but originated in Africa. This annual plant has a horizontal stem. The skin may be pale or dark green and flesh is normally red to pink, though orange-fleshed varieties exist. The numerous flat seeds are usually black. True to its name, the watermelon has a high water content (92–95 percent). It has been eaten since antiquity around the Mediterranean and in Egypt, and is grown in the subtropical countries, including the southern United States. Watermelon contains vitamin C and potassium. It has purifying, diuretic, and detoxifying properties.

Watermelon mozza

1 | Peel the watermelon, and cut it into 4 slices ⅝ inch (15 mm) thick. Cut 4 rectangles out of each slice, using a rectangular cutter measuring 3 x 1½ inches (7½ x 3½ cm).

2 | Tear the mozzarella into 16 pieces.

3 | Rinse a plate under cold water. Place a rectangle of watermelon on it, then 4 pieces of mozzarella, 3 basil leaves, and a few daikon sprouts. Season with salt and pepper and sprinkle with a little olive oil. Serve immediately.

Recommended wine: Laurent-Perrier Brut pink champagne.

Serves 4

½ watermelon
1 ball of mozzarella
12 purple basil leaves
Daikon sprouts
Sea salt
Freshly ground black pepper
Extra-virgin olive oil (preferably Manni)

Serves 4

1 mango
½ orange bell pepper
1 watermelon
12 borage flowers
4 sprigs chervil
8 chives
Daikon sprouts
Sea salt
Freshly ground black pepper
Extra-virgin olive oil

Watermelon
ikebana

1 | Purée the mango and bell pepper
separately. Put the two purées aside in
the refrigerator.

2 | Peel the watermelon and cut it into
4 slices ⅝ inch (15 mm) thick.
Cut 4 rectangles out of each slice, using
a rectangular cookie cutter measuring
3 x 1¼ inches (7½ x 3½ cm).

3 | On a plate, arrange a watermelon
rectangle, 3 borage flowers, 1 musky
chervil sprig, 2 chives, and a few daikon
sprouts. Spread a trail of mango purée
beside the watermelon rectangle and dot
with a little bell-pepper purée. Season
with salt and pepper and sprinkle with
a little olive oil. Serve immediately.

Recommended wine: Champagne
Demi-sec Veuve-Cliquot.

Serves 4

Prepare the iced meringue the night before
12 egg whites
1 vanilla bean
1 tablespoon orange
   flower water
2½ tbsp granulated sugar
1 watermelon
1 passion fruit

Iced watermelon and passion fruit meringue

1 | The night before, beat the eggs gradually to stiff peaks. Scrape out the vanilla bean. Gradually fold the vanilla seeds into the egg whites, along with the orange flower water and sugar. Cover a serving platter with plastic wrap. Arrange 4 4-inch (10-cm) hoops on the platter and fill them with the meringue. Place in the freezer.

2 | On the day itself, cut out a large slice of watermelon ¾ inch (20 mm) thick and cut out 4 rounds, using a hoop.

3 | Place 1 watermelon round on each of 4 chilled plates. Unmold the meringues by dipping a knife in warm water and running it round the inside of the molds. Place a meringue on top of each watermelon round. Garnish with a trail of passion-fruit juice around the rings and place ¼ of a vanilla bean on top.

Recommended wine: Muscat de Rivesaltes 2001, Domaine de Blanes (M.-P. Bories).

Garden peas, grapefruit, and peppermint— a crunchy juice

1 | Peel 1 grapefruit, discarding all white parts. Remove skin from the segments and divide them into 3. Squeeze the juice from the second grapefruit. Mix them with the shelled garden peas and 12 chopped peppermint leaves. Sprinkle with a little olive oil. Leave to marinate for 30 minutes.

2 | Divide the peas and grapefruit pieces between 4 glasses. Sprinkle with the juice and a little olive oil.

This makes a delicious appetizer or aperitive.

Serves 4

2 grapefruit
9 oz (250 g) very fresh
   garden peas
12 peppermint leaves
Extra-virgin olive oil

Stuffed zucchini blossoms
with garden pea tzatziki

1 | Dice the cucumber into ¼-inch (5-mm) cubes.

2 | Finely chop the mint leaves.

3 | Shell the peas.

4 | Pour the yogurt into a large bowl. Mix it with the cucumber, mint, garden peas, green onion flowers, and a little olive oil. Season with salt and pepper.

5 | Divide the tzatziki (cucumber and yogurt mixture) between the 4 zucchini blossoms and sprinkle with a little olive oil.

Recommended wine: Côtes-du-Luberon Rosé 1999.

Serves 4

1 cucumber
12 mint leaves
9 oz (250 g) garden peas
9 oz (200 g) Greek yogurt
20 green onion flowers
Extra-virgin olive oil
Sea salt
Freshly ground black pepper
4 zucchini blossoms

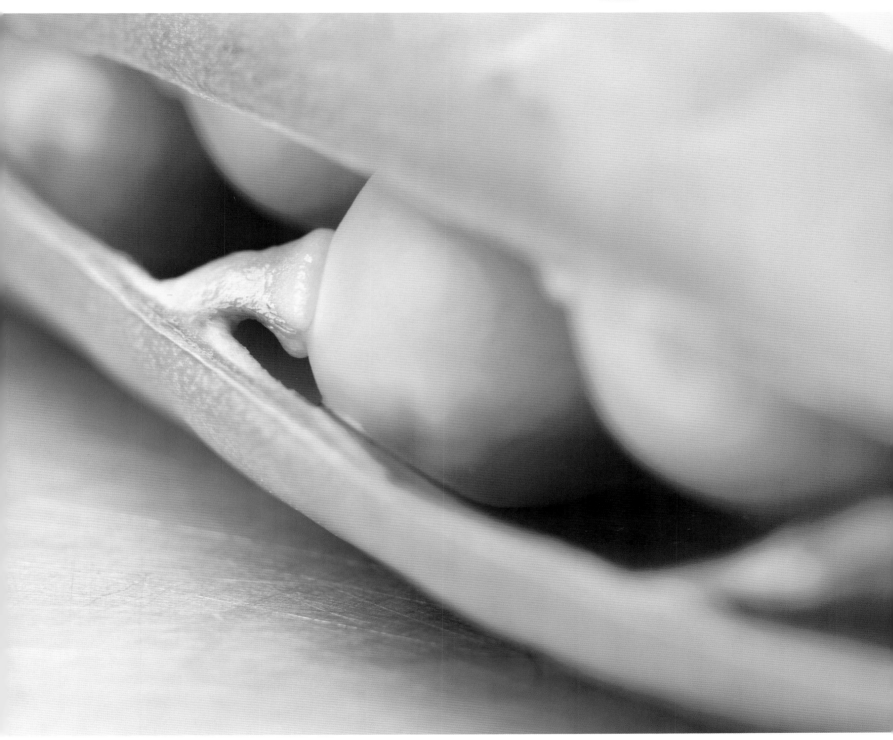

GARDEN PEA, from the Latin *pisum*, itself from the Greek *pisos*. The pea is the seed of the climbing garden plant with pretty white flowers; the edible green seeds are contained inside a long pod. The pea plant is a legume, the product of centuries of cultivation and selection, of which there are now over a thousand varieties. Numerous vestiges of the plant, including pods containing peas more than 10,000 years old, have been found in Anatolia, Iran, Greece, and Israel. The pea probably originated in the Middle East, India or Persia. Its importation into Europe probably dates from around the same time. The pea was brought from Italy to the court of King Louis XIV of France, who immediately expressed a liking for it. The favor bestowed by the king on the plant gave it such prestige that it became the most prized of all the vegetables grown at Versailles. The garden pea is rich in vitamins, protein, and carbohydrates.

Serves 4

1lb 2 oz (500 g) very fresh
   garden peas
7 fl oz (200 ml) coconut milk
16 mint leaves
Extra-virgin olive oil
Sea salt
Ground black pepper
5 fl oz (150 ml) whipping
   cream
4 coriander flowers
4 red orach leaves

Garden pea soup
with coconut milk
and coriander flowers

1 | Shell the peas and combine them in a food processor with the coconut milk, 12 mint leaves, and a sprinkling of olive oil. Season with salt and pepper. Strain the mixture through a fine sieve and chill until required.

2 | Beat the cream until stiff. Chill until required.

3 | Fill each glass two-thirds full with the pea mixture. Top with the whipped cream, 1 coriander flower, 1 mint leaf, and 1 red orach leaf. Drizzle with olive oil. Serve immediately.

Recommended wine: White Riesling 1998, Grand Cru Eichberg (O. & D. Weber).

Pear

Pear, corn, and duck tartare

Serves 4

2 pears
Juice of 1 lemon
1 duck breast
Aged balsamic vinegar
Sea salt
2 tablespoons hazelnut oil
1 tablespoon soy sauce
1 corn cob
16 mint leaves, chopped
4 green onions (scallions)
1 tablespoon aged
  balsamic vinegar
Ground black pepper

1 | Shell the corn cob.

2 | Use a mandoline to cut half a pear into 4 thin slices. Then cut the rest of the pears into ¼-inch (5-mm) cubes. Sprinkle with lemon juice and chill until required.

3 | Slice the duck breast into ¼-inch (5-mm) cubes (the size of a grain of corn), discarding the skin. Chill until required.

4 | Dissolve the salt in the white balsamic vinegar. Emulsify with the hazelnut oil and soy sauce. Set aside.

5 | In a large bowl, combine the corn with the cubes of pear, duck, chopped mint, and vinegar mixture.

6 | Chill 4 serving plates. Place a rectangular cookie cutter measuring 3 x 1¼ inches (7½ x 3½ cm) on each plate and fill with the mixture. Unmold. Top the assembly with 1 slice of pear, 1 mint leaf, 1 green onion (scallion), and a drizzle of aged balsamic vinegar.

Recommended wine:
Riesling Vieilles Vignes 1999 (Charles Frey).

PEAR from the vulgar Latin *pira*, plural of the classical Latin *pirum*. The cultivation of the pear dates from prehistoric times. It originated in central Asia and was already cultivated three thousand years ago. The pear tree grows in temperate regions. The fruit was highly prized by the Egyptians, Romans, and ancient Chinese. There are hundreds of varieties of pear today, most of which are the result of hybrids produced in the seventeenth and eighteenth centuries. The pear is rich in fiber and contains traces of potassium and copper, both essential to human life. It has diuretic and sedative properties.

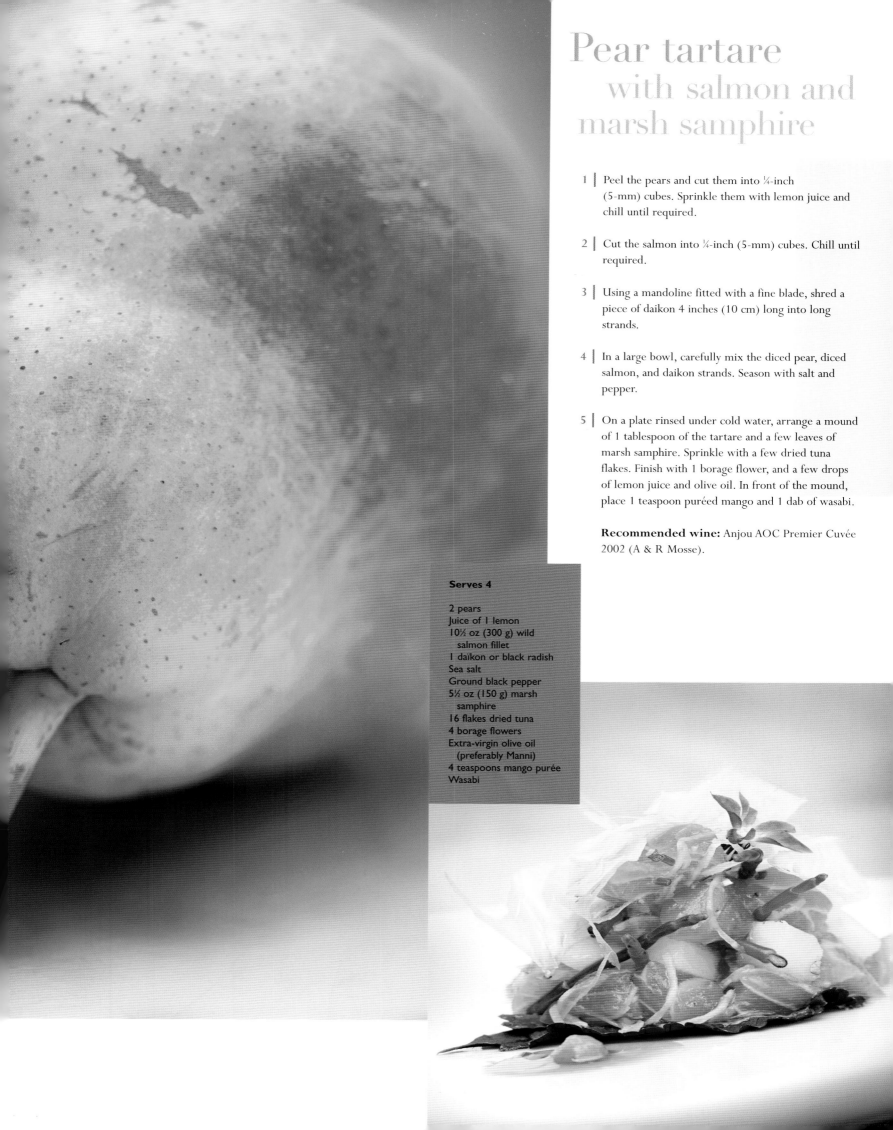

Pear tartare
with salmon and marsh samphire

1 | Peel the pears and cut them into ¼-inch
(5-mm) cubes. Sprinkle them with lemon juice and
chill until required.

2 | Cut the salmon into ¼-inch (5-mm) cubes. Chill until
required.

3 | Using a mandoline fitted with a fine blade, shred a
piece of daikon 4 inches (10 cm) long into long
strands.

4 | In a large bowl, carefully mix the diced pear, diced
salmon, and daikon strands. Season with salt and
pepper.

5 | On a plate rinsed under cold water, arrange a mound
of 1 tablespoon of the tartare and a few leaves of
marsh samphire. Sprinkle with a few dried tuna
flakes. Finish with 1 borage flower, and a few drops
of lemon juice and olive oil. In front of the mound,
place 1 teaspoon puréed mango and 1 dab of wasabi.

Recommended wine: Anjou AOC Premier Cuvée
2002 (A & R Mosse).

Serves 4

2 pears
Juice of 1 lemon
10½ oz (300 g) wild
  salmon fillet
1 daïkon or black radish
Sea salt
Ground black pepper
5½ oz (150 g) marsh
  samphire
16 flakes dried tuna
4 borage flowers
Extra-virgin olive oil
  (preferably Manni)
4 teaspoons mango purée
Wasabi

Pear, duck, and red cabbage salad

1 | Without peeling, slice 1 pear on the mandoline into thin slices. Peel the other pear, core it, and dice it into ¼-inch (5-mm) cubes. Sprinkle with lemon juice and chill until required.

2 | Using the mandoline, shred the half red cabbage into thin rounds. Chill until required.

3 | Dissolve the salt in the aged wine vinegar. Emulsify in a blender with the olive oil and maple syrup. Set it aside.

4 | Chop the fennel stems into ½-inch (1-cm) pieces.

5 | In a large bowl, toss the red cabbage, diced pear, capers, fennel, and redcurrants. Season lightly.

6 | Take a plate rinsed under cold water and arrange a mound of the mixture on it. Around the mound, place alternate slices of pear and cured duck. Pour a trail of the vinaigrette dressing and a little mango and melon purée around.

Recommended wine: Corbières Rosé 2001.

Serves 4

2 Bartlett pears
Juice of 1 lemon
½ red cabbage
1 tablespoon aged
  wine vinegar
Sea salt
2 tablespoons
  extra-virgin olive oil
1 teaspoon maple
  syrup
2 fennel stems
16 capers
30 reducurrants
Ground black pepper
20 slices cured duck
  (see recipe page 64)
2 tablespoons mango
  purée
2 tablespoons melon
  purée

Bell pepper
and caviar bites

Serves 4

1 green bell pepper
1 red bell pepper
1 orange bell pepper
1 yellow bell pepper
1 cauliflower
1 pear
3½ oz (100 g) caviar
Aged balsamic vinegar
Extra-virgin olive oil

1 | Dice all of the bell peppers, the cauliflower, and the pear into ¼-inch (5-mm) cubes. Set them aside.

2 | On a plate, arrange a line consisting of a teaspoon of green bell pepper, a teaspoon of red bell pepper, a teaspoon of orange bell pepper, a teaspoon of yellow bell pepper, a teaspoon of pear, and a teaspoon of cauliflower. On each vegetable mound, place a few caviar eggs, and sprinkle with a few drops of olive oil and balsamic vinegar. Serve immediately.

Recommended wine: Champagne Gosset 1995.

Bell pepper,
tomato, and feta cheese gazpacho

Serves 4

Make the gazpacho the night before
1 red bell pepper
3 tomatoes
½ cucumber
1 shallot
1 garlic clove
Extra-virgin olive oil
Sea salt
Freshly ground black pepper
6 slices cured duck
   (see recipe page 64)
4½ oz (125 g) feta cheese
Tarragon

1 | The night before, mix the bell pepper, tomatoes, cucumber, shallot, garlic clove, and a little olive oil in a food processor. Season with salt and pepper. Strain the mixture through a fine sieve. Chill until required.

2 | On the day itself, slice the cured duck into small matchstick strips.

3 | Tear the feta into small pieces.

4 | Pour the gazpacho into a soup bowl. Sprinkle it with feta, the matchstick strips of cured duck, and the tarragon. Sprinkle with a little olive oil. Serve immediately.

Recommended wine: Irouléguy 1996, Domaine Brana.

Bell pepper

BELL PEPPER, from the Latin *piper, -eris* , the fruit of the pepper tree. In fact, the bell pepper (so-called because of its bell shape) or sweet pepper *Capsicum annum*, is a member of the Capsaceae family, the pimento, a New World plant completely unrelated to the pepper tree. It is an annual that produces a shiny fruit whose colors range from yellow to purple. The fruit is usually bell-shaped or conical, and may be more or less "peppery" depending on the variety. Pimentos have been eaten in Mexico since 7,000 BCE. The first cultivated varieties date from at least 5,000 BCE, making this vegetable one of the first to be cultivated as a crop on the American continent. Christopher Columbus was the first to call the plant a "pepper"; one of the aims of his voyage had been to bring the precious spice back with him from the East Indies. Capsicums are particularly rich in vitamin C, and bell pepper also contains vitamins B_1 and B_2.

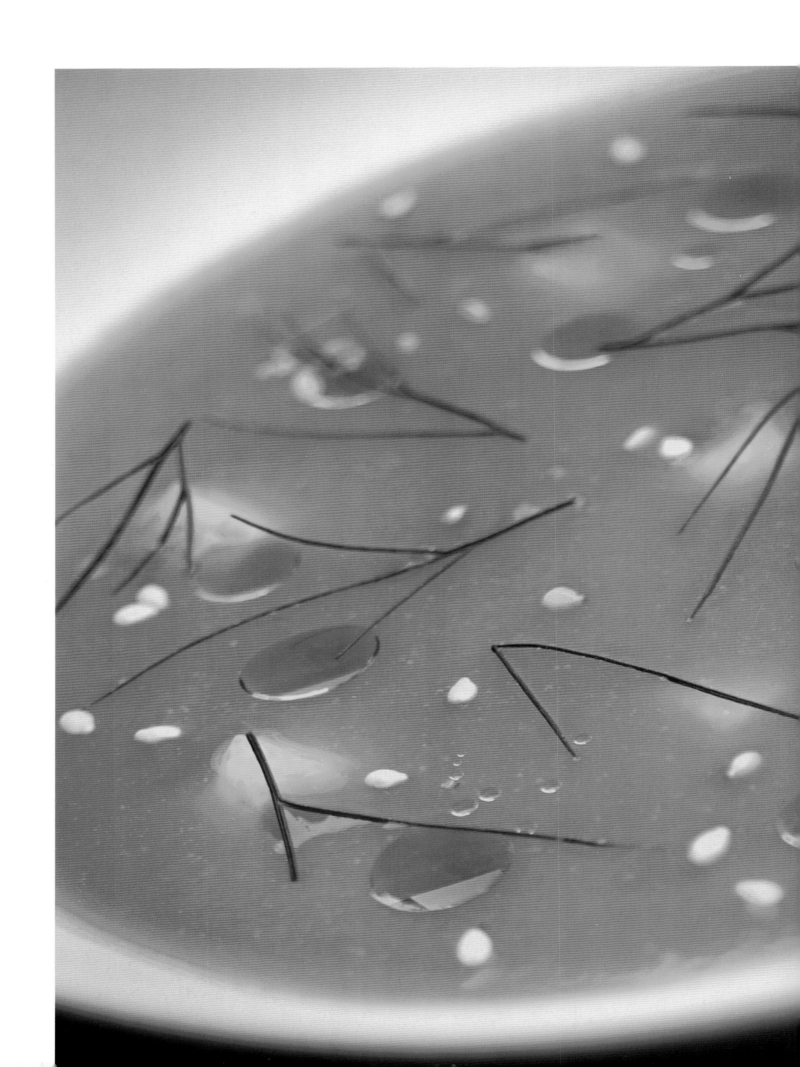

Serves 4

1 Victoria pineapple
8 red bell peppers
1 teaspoon maple syrup
Sea salt
White balsamic vinegar
Freshly ground black
  pepper
12 fennel fronds
Extra-virgin olive oil

Bell pepper
and victoria pineapple
fruit soup

1 | Peel the pineapple and dice it into ¼-inch (5-mm) cubes. Chill until required.

2 | Process the peppers in a food processor. Combine the juice obtained with the maple syrup, a pinch of salt, and a drizzle of white balsamic vinegar. Season with pepper.

3 | Divide the pepper soup between four bowls. Sprinkle it with the cubes of pineapple and fennel fronds. Sprinkle with a few drops of olive oil. Serve immediately.

Recommended wine: Brut Rosé 1999, Cà-del-Bosco (Italy).

Pomelo and raspberries in a beet granita

1 | Two hours before serving, place the beet juice in the freezer. Every 30 minutes, fork over the beet juice in order to break up into ice crystals.

2 | Mix the honey and wasabi, and set aside the mixture.

3 | Peel the pomelo, discarding the pith, and break up into segments. Remove the skin from the segments.

4 | In a cocktail glass, arrange a few pieces of pomelo and 5 raspberries, and cover with the beet crystals. Finish with a few drops of the honey sauce. Serve immediately.

Recommended wine: Sainte-Croix-du-Mont 2002.

Serves 4

7 fl oz (200 ml) beet juice
1 tablespoon liquid honey
1 teaspoon wasabi
2 pomelo
20 raspberries

Pomelo, fromage blanc, maple syrup, and basil leaves

1 | In a small bowl, mix the fromage blanc with 2 tablespoons of maple syrup. Chill until required.

2 | Peel the pomelo, discarding the pith, and break it into segments. Remove the skin from the segments.

3 | Spread 2 tablespoons of the cheese mixture on a plate. Place 3 pomelo segments on it. Intersperse each with 1 purple basil leaf. Sprinkle with the broken pistachios, then with a few drops of maple syrup.

Recommended wine: Coteaux-du-Layou Villages 2001.

Serves 4

7 oz (200 g) fromage blanc
Maple syrup
2 pomelos
12 purple basil leaves
2 tablespoons chopped
    pistachios

Pomelo

POMELO, PUMMELO, from the Latin *pomum*, a fruit. The pomelo (*Citrus grandis*) originated in Malaysia and Indonesia, where it was discovered by a Captain Shaddock, who first brought the seeds to the West Indies—the fruit is also known as shaddock after him. It is almost certainly a relation of the grapefruit (*Citrus paradisi*) which was first found growing in Jamaica in 1850, the other member of the family being the citron (*Citrus medica*). The pomelo is a large, round fruit that grows in bunches like a grapefruit. The skin and pulp may be yellow, pink, or red, and the flavor is slightly bitter. It has the same thick pith as a citron. The nutritional value depends on the color, the pink and blood-red varieties having a slightly higher vitamin A content. The pomelo also contains vitamin C, potassium, and folic acid. It stimulates the appetite and has digestive, antiseptic, and diuretic properties.

Carpaccio of pomelo and sea bass

1 | Wrap the bass fillets in plastic wrap and leave them in the freezer for 30 minutes.

2 | Peel the pomelo, discarding the pith, and carefully separate the segments. Remove the skin from the segments and break them up. Peel the kiwi fruit, slice it, and break the slices into pieces. Chill until required.

3 | Remove the bass from the freezer and slice it very thinly using an electric slicer.

4 | Rinse a plate under cold water and cover it with pomelo and kiwi pieces. Arrange a few thin slices of bass and 1 chopped shiso leaf on the fruit. Sprinkle with lime zest.

Recommended wine: Bellet Blanc 2001.

Serves 4

2 bass fillets
1 pomelo
1 kiwi fruit
4 shiso leaves
Zest of 1 lime

Green apple

APPLE, from the Old English *aeppel*, related to Old Saxon *appel*. Its Latin name, *pomum*, was originally used to designate the edible fruit of any tree. The fruit of the apple tree, one of the oldest and most extensively cultivated of trees, originated in southwest Asia. Archeological excavations have shown that the original wild apple grew in prehistoric Europe. By the sixth century BCE, thirty-seven varieties were known to the Romans. They contributed to the spread of the fruit, introducing it to England and across Europe. In about 1620, the first colonists brought the apple to North America. Today, there are more than 7,500 varieties. The Granny Smith is a variety that originated in Australia, where it was first grown in 1868—by a grandmother named Smith, not surprisingly. It is a late-fruiting variety of average size that is green, juicy, and acidic. Most of the nutrients in the apple (vitamin C, potassium) lie just beneath the skin. Eating a raw apple cleans the teeth and massages the gums.

Red cabbage, smoked herring, and Granny Smith matchsticks

Serves 4

1 teaspoon cider vinegar
Sea salt
2 tablespoons hazelnut oil
1 teaspoon grainy French mustard
Coriander seeds
Fennel seeds
Freshly ground black pepper
1 red cabbage
2 Granny Smith apples
Juice of 1 lemon
7 oz (200 g) smoked herring

1 | Dissolve the salt in the cider vinegar. Blend with the hazelnut oil, mustard, and a pinch of the coriander and fennel seeds, reserving some for the garnish. Season with pepper and set aside.

2 | Using a mandoline, cut the red cabbage into thin slices.

3 | Wash the apples and cut them into ¼-inch (5-mm) thick matchstick strips. Sprinkle them with lemon juice.

4 | Cut the smoked herring into ½-inch (1-cm) cubes.

5 | Toss the mixture lightly to blend.

6 | Arrange a mound of the mixture on each plate. Add a trail of the dressing and sprinkle with a few coriander and fennel seeds.

Recommended wine: Ménetou-Salon 2002, Château de Maupas.

Serves 4

2 Granny Smith apples
Juice of 1 lemon
4 teaspoons salmon roe

Granny Smith and salmon roe—a crunchy juice

1 | Process the green apples in a food processor. Transfer them to a bowl and sprinkle lightly with lemon juice.

2 | Rinse 4 glasses in cold running water. Divide the apple juice between them and add 1 teaspoon salmon roe per glass.

This is makes a novel aperitif or appetizer.

Granny Smith spaghetti with salmon tartare

1 | Dissolve the salt in the balsamic vinegar. Emulsify it with the olive oil and soy sauce. Season with pepper and set aside.

2 | Dice the salmon into ½-inch (1-cm) cubes. Chill until required.

3 | Use a vegetable mill to shred 3 apples into spaghetti-like strands. Sprinkle with lemon juice. Use a mandoline to slice the fourth apple into 4 thin slices. Sprinkle with lemon juice.

4 | Rinse a plate under cold water. With a fork, curl a spiral of apple strands. Place 1 slice of apple on top. Top with 1 teaspoon of trout roe. Beside this, arrange a few salmon cubes topped with 3 chive flowers. Finish the dish with a drizzle of vinaigrette.

Recommended wine: Haut-Poitou Rosé 2002.

Serves 4

1 teaspoon balsamic
  vinegar
Sea salt
2 tablespoons extra-virgin
  olive oil
1 teaspoon soy sauce
Pepper
7 oz (200 g) wild salmon
  fillet
4 Granny Smith apples
Juice of 1 lemon
4 teaspoons trout roe
12 chive flowers

Salmon and melon sushi

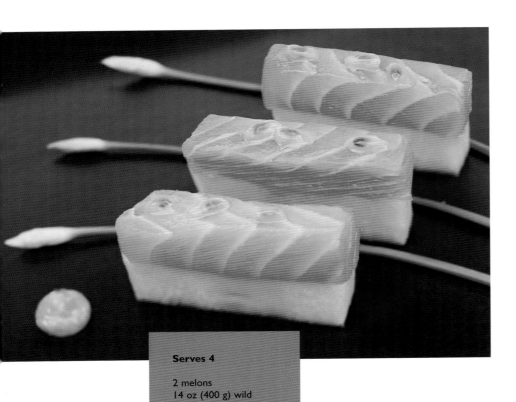

1 | From the melon, cut 12 large "French fries," 2¾ inches (7 cm) long by 1¼ inches (3 cm) wide and ½ inch (1.5 cm) thick.

2 | Do the same with the salmon.

3 | Rinse a plate under cold water, and place 3 melon fries on it, topped with 3 salmon fries. Add a teaspoon of passion fruit. Arrange the Chinese chives in between the fries. On one side, add a dab of wasabi.

Recommended wine: Jurançon Sec, 2002.

Serves 4

2 melons
14 oz (400 g) wild salmon fillet
1 passion fruit
12 Chinese chives
Wasabi

Salmon tartare
in a fennel shell

1 | Clean the fennel bulbs, reserving the 4 outer layers to make shells, and leaving on 3½ inches (9 cm) of the stem. Put them in a bowl of water containing ice cubes. Cut the rest of the fennel bulbs into ¼-inch (5-mm) cubes. Chill until required.

2 | Cut the salmon into ½ inch (1-cm) cubes.

3 | In a salad bowl, carefully mix the fennel cubes, salmon, passion fruit, chopped shiso leaves, a little olive oil, and the juice and grated rind of the lime. Season with salt and pepper.

4 | On a plate rinsed in cold water, place 1 well-dried fennel shell, and fill it with the tartare mixture. Top with 1 Japanese chive. Serve immediately.

Recommended wine: Auxey-Duresses Blanc, 2000.

Serves 4

4 fennel bulbs
14 oz (400 g) wild salmon fillet
1 passion fruit
8 shiso leaves, chopped
Extra-virgin olive oil
1 lime
Sea salt
Freshly ground black pepper
4 Japanese chives

Salmon

SALMON, from the Latin *salmo, -onis*. This pink-fleshed, oily fish has been highly prized since antiquity for its flesh and the pleasure it brings to the fisherman. There are six species of salmon—five in the Pacific and one in the Atlantic—and a sub-species that lives in fresh water. This large fish feeds in the sea but swims upriver to reproduce in the spawning ground in which it was born. The salmon is nowadays threatened with intensive fishing, pollution, and in some countries also by the construction of dams on its native rivers. The Pacific salmon owes its survival to fish-farming and strict regulation of the existing reserves, as well as to the "fish-ladders" inserted into dams that enable it to reach home despite the obstacles. The fish is rich in protein and omega-3 oils.

Serves 4

1 tablespoon liquid honey
2 teaspoons soy sauce
10½ oz (300 g) wild
  salmon fillet
2 cucumbers
4 teaspoons salmon roe
20 marsh samphire stems
Extra-virgin olive oil
  (preferably Manni)
Wasabi

Salmon, cucumber, and marsh samphire spring roll

1 │ Combine the honey and soy sauce, and set the mixture aside.

2 │ Cut the salmon into ¼-inch (5-mm) cubes. Chill until required.

3 │ Using a mandoline, slice the cucumbers into 12 ribbons.

4 │ On a plate, shape the cucumbers into 3 rolls. Fill them two-thirds
full with the diced salmon. Top with 1 teaspoon salmon roe and
1 bunch of marsh samphire. Sprinkle with a few drops of olive oil.
In front of each arrangement, place 1 teaspoon of the honey–soy
sauce mixture and one dab of wasabi.

Recommended wine: Graves Blanc 2001.

Soy

SOYA, SOY from the Manchu *soya*. Soya is the most nutritional and unusual of legumes, an annual and herbaceous bean similar to the green bean. It originated in China, where it has been cultivated for five millennia. It was introduced to France by missionaries in about 1740. It has only been cultivated in Europe since the late nineteenth century, and it has never had the importance that it acquired in the United States, which is one of the world's largest producers of soya. Soybeans are the richest source of plant protein known to man, and they also contain 15–20 percent fat. Soybeans are absolute record breakers in calorie content; they also contain all the amino acids needed by the human organism, and all of the B vitamins. The only problem is that, in its raw form, the soybean is poisonous and also highly indigestible, and needs 24 hours of cooking before it can be eaten. Soybean sprouts can be eaten raw, however. If they are not available, the sprouts of the mung bean (*Vigna mungo*) can be substituted.

Serves 4

4 spring roll wrappers
  measuring 7 inches
  (18cm) in diameter
7oz (200g) soybean
  sprouts
4 coriander sprigs
4 mint sprigs
4 chervil sprigs
Juice of 2 limes
1 tablespoon white
  sesame seeds
Sea salt and pepper
Olive oil
4 blood oranges
3 tablespoons honey
Soy sauce
6 lumps Muscovado sugar

Soybean sprout spring roll and herb salad with muscovado sugar, honey, and blood-orange juice

1 | Soak the spring roll wrappers in cold water until they soften. Remove them from the water and drain them on a dry kitchen towel, then cover them with another to absorb the excess water.

2 | In the center of a wrapper place a quarter of the soybean sprouts with 1 leaf of each herb (coriander, mint, chervil), a few drops of lime juice, and a pinch of sesame seeds.

3 | Make a spring roll by rolling up the wrapper and folding one end toward the center.

4 | Separate the rest of the herbs and season them at the last moment with a few grains of sea salt, 2–3 turns of the pepper mill, the rest of the lime juice, and olive oil.

5 | Squeeze the oranges, discarding the seeds and leaving the little pieces of pulp in it so that the juice is fairly thick.

6 | Use the soy sauce to liquefy the honey. The flavor of the sauce should not be masked by the soy sauce.

7 | On a plate, arrange 1 spring roll and a quarter of the herb salad. Lightly crush the sugar lumps in a mortar and sprinkle the herb salad with them.

8 | Pour the honey–soy sauce mixture over the whole dish and sprinkle the spring rolls with sesame seeds. Serve the chilled blood-orange juice separately in a small glass.

Soy tabbouleh

1 | Trim the tiny roots from the soybean sprouts. Dice the soybean sprouts so that they are the same size as grains of bulgur wheat, one of the main ingredients in tabbouleh. Lightly sprinkle with lemon juice to prevent the sprouts from darkening.

2 | Mince the flat-leaved parsley.

3 | Cut the tomatoes into quarters and scoop out the insides, carefully reserving them. Chop the tomato flesh into cubes.

4 | Combine the interiors and tomato flesh with the rest of the soybeans (adding a little water to liquefy if necessary). Strain through a conical sieve. Season to taste with salt, pepper, Tabasco, lemon juice, and olive oil. Chill until required.

5 | Combine the beansprout bulgur, diced tomato, and chopped parsley, and season in the same way as the soy-and-tomato shot with salt, pepper, Tabasco, lemon juice, and olive oil to taste. Chill until required. Do not mix in advance with the beansprouts, which will lose their crunchiness if combined too early with salt and the acidity of the lemon and tomato juices.

6 | When ready to serve, place the tabbouleh in individual bowls or a large salad dish. Serve the chilled soy–tomato mixture on the side (it will accentuate the refreshing nature of the dish).

Recommended wine: Coteaux-d'Aix-en-Provence Rosé 2002.

Serves 4

12 oz (350 g) soybean sprouts for the tabbouleh
3 oz (80 g) soybean sprouts for the drinking juice
3–4 lemons
2 bunches flat-leaved parsley
6 tomatoes, preferably Roma (4 firm slices for the tabbouleh and 2 for the drinking juice)
Sea salt
Pepper
Tabasco
Extra-virgin olive oil

Serves 4

12 medium langoustines
14 fl oz (400 ml) soy milk
Sea salt
Pepper
12 lemon balm leaves
12 basil leaves
12 coriander leaves
7 oz (200 g) soybean sprouts
3 limes
Tabasco
4 passion fruit
Extra-virgin olive oil

Soy rolled in langoustine carpaccio with soy and passion-fruit milk

1 | Shell the langoustines. Crush the pincers and heads and soak them in the soy milk in a cool place until it is sufficiently impregnated with langoustine flavor, then strain through a conical sieve.

2 | Slice the langoustine flesh. Flatten the pieces and season with salt and pepper. Arrange a leaf of each herb on top of each piece of langoustine. Trim the soybean sprouts and add a little bunch of them. Roll them into a ring and chill until required.

3 | Season the soy–langoustine milkshake with the lime juice (it will thicken the milk), and salt, pepper, and Tabasco.

4 | Cut open the passion fruit and scoop out the flesh. Season it with olive oil, Tabasco, salt, and pepper.

5 | On each plate, arrange 3 soybean–langoustine pieces and sprinkle them with seasoned passion-fruit pulp. Serve with 4 glasses of soy–langoustine milk and place a little passion-fruit flesh on each plate.

Recommended wine: Clairette du Languedoc, 2002.

Serves 4

1 melon
1 watermelon
12 oz (350 g) tuna fillet
Daikon sprouts
Chive flowers
Coriander flowers
Aged balsamic vinegar
Mango juice

TUNA, from the Latin *Thunnus*, a large fish. The tuna and related species (bonito, albacore, and skipjack) swim in the warm waters of the Mediterranean, Pacific, Atlantic, and the Indian Ocean. The fish is warm-blooded and requires large amounts of oxygen, so it swims fast. This oily fish has dark red flesh that is particularly nutritious when raw and loses some of its value when canned. Raw tuna is highly prized by the Japanese and is eaten in sashimi. In addition to fats, it contains potassium and other trace elements.

Tuna

Fruit sandwich with tuna

1 | Cut out 4 rectangles of melon and watermelon, using a rectangular 3 x 1¼-inch (7.5 x 3.5-cm) cookie cutter. Set aside in a cool place.

2 | Cut the tuna into ⅜-inch (8-mm) cubes. Set aside.

3 | On a plate rinsed under cold water, use a rectangular cookie cutter or mold to assemble 1 rectangle of watermelon, 1 layer of tuna, and 1 rectangle of melon. Finish with a few daikon sprouts, chive flowers, and coriander flowers. Trace a trail of balsamic vinegar and mango juice in front of the "sandwiches."

Recommended wine: Bandol Rosé 2002.

Tuna turkish delight

1 | Cut the tuna into ¼-inch (2-cm) cubes. Use a brush to glaze 5 sides of each cube with aged balsamic vinegar. Sprinkle the glazed sides with white sesame seeds.

2 | Shred the daikon into long vermicelli-like strips, using a mandoline with fine blades.

3 | Rinse a plate with cold water, and arrange the tuna Turkish delights on it with the unglazed side on top. Place 1 passion-fruit seed in its flesh on each one. Beside them, arrange a bunch of daikon strands, 1 borage flower, and a hazelnut-sized dab of wasabi.

Recommended wine: Tokay d'Alsace 2002.

Serves 4

12 oz (350 g) tuna fillet
Aged balsamic vinegar
White sesame seeds
1 daïkon (or black radish)
1 passion fruit
4 borage flowers
Wasabi

Serves 4

1 avocado
1 teaspoon lemon juice
Extra-virgin olive oil
Sea salt
Freshly ground black
    pepper
1 mango
14 oz (400 g) tuna fillet
4 wild asparagus spears
16 enoki mushrooms
4 chives
Chive flowers
Coriander flowers
1 passion fruit

Tuna and two purées

1 | In the blender process the avocado, lemon juice, and a sprinkling
    of olive oil. Season with salt and pepper. Refrigerate.

2 | Process the mango with salt and pepper. Refrigerate.

3 | Slice the tuna fillet into 4 pieces.

4 | On a plate rinsed under cold water, arrange 1 piece of tuna,
    1 spear of wild asparagus, 4 enoki mushrooms, and 1 strand of
    chive. Sprinkle with a few chive and coriander flowers. Place
    1 tablespoon of avocado purée on one side of the tuna, and 1
    tablespoon of mango purée on the other. Add a few passion-fruit
    seeds and flesh. Sprinkle with a few drops of olive oil.

Recommended wine: Bugey Blanc 2002.

Green zebra soup, salmon, and cottage cheese

1 | In a bowl, use a fork to mix the fromage frais, chopped chives, and a little olive oil. Season with salt and pepper.

2 | Cut the salmon escalopes into squares measuring 3¼ x 3¼ inches (8 x 8 cm). In the center of each, place 2 teaspoons fromage frais. Fold the squares over the fromage frais to make pillows. Chill until required.

3 | In the blender, process the tomatoes with a little olive oil. Season with salt and pepper. Strain through a fine sieve.

4 | Place a salmon pillow in a shallow bowl. Pour the tomato soup around it until it is half submerged. Grind pepper over it. Serve immediately.

Recommended wine: Rosé de Grammenon, 2003 (M. Aubéry-Clément).

Serves 4

4 tablespoons fromage
   frais
1 tablespoon chopped
   chives
Extra-virgin olive oil
Salt and freshly ground
   black pepper
4 thin slices salmon
10 green tomatoes
   (preferably Green Zebra)

Tomato and watermelon salad; melon juice to drink

1 | Process the melon in the blender. Sprinkle with lemon juice and chill until required.

2 | Deseed the tomatoes and cut them into ¼-inch (5-mm) cubes.

3 | Do the same with the watermelon until you have an equal quantity of cubes.

4 | Chop the equivalent of 1 tablespoon celery into ¼-inch (5-mm) cubes.

5 | In a bowl, carefully combine the cubes of tomato, watermelon, and celery, and add 1 tablespoon olive oil. Season with salt and pepper.

6 | On a plate rinsed under cold water, place a square cookie cutter measuring 3¼ x 3¼ inches (8 x 8 cm), and fill with the salad. Sprinkle with a few chopped celery leaves and a little olive oil. Serve immediately with a glass of melon juice.

Serves 4

1 melon
Juice of 1 lemon
2 beefsteak tomatoes
1 watermelon
1 celery stalk with
   leaves
Extra-virgin olive oil
Sea salt
Freshly ground black
   pepper

TOMATO, from the Spanish *tomate* and the Aztec *tomatl*. There are more than one thousand varieties of this annual herbaceous plant of the Solanaceae family. Archeological excavation has revealed that the tomato was cultivated in the coastal plains of Peru centuries before the Spanish conquest of South America in the sixteenth century. The conquistadors described it as a mandrake, another member of the same family which, like deadly nightshade (another solanum), is fatal if eaten in large quantities (although it is used as a medicine in minute amounts). For this reason, the tomato was "quarantined" for almost two centuries. The tomato is very rich in minerals, especially potassium, trace elements, vitamin A, folic acid, and vitamin C. The tomato is also said to have medicinal properties and has been used to treat skin and eye infections. Today, since it is an antioxidant, it is said to help prevent cancer.

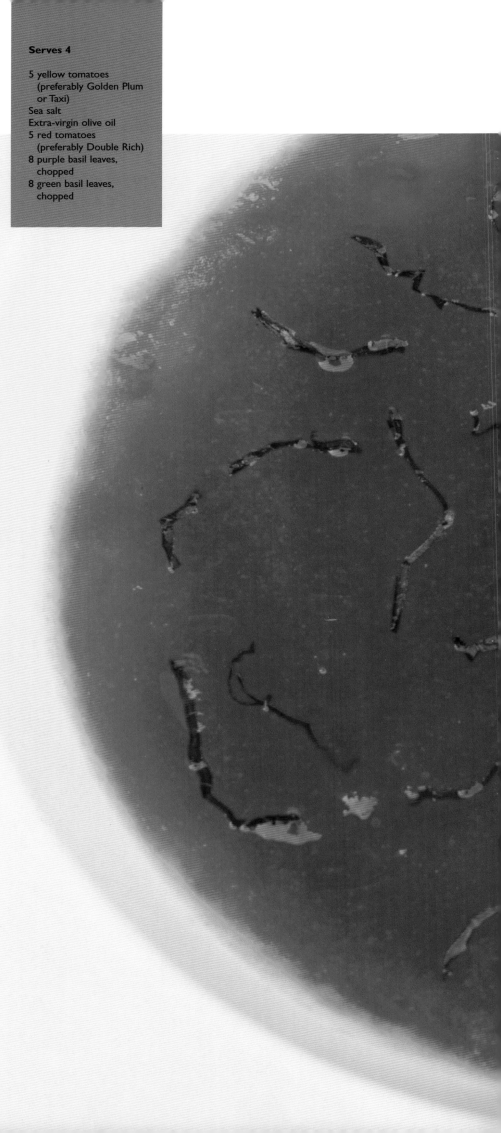

Serves 4

5 yellow tomatoes
(preferably Golden Plum
or Taxi)
Sea salt
Extra-virgin olive oil
5 red tomatoes
(preferably Double Rich)
8 purple basil leaves,
chopped
8 green basil leaves,
chopped

Yin and yang
golden plum and double rich tomato soup

1 | Deseed the yellow tomatoes. Process the flesh in a blender with a pinch of salt and a sprinkling of olive oil. Strain the soup through a fine strainer.

2 | Do the same with the red tomatoes.

3 | Into a rinsed bowl, pour a tablespoon of each tomato soup without letting them mix. Sprinkle the yellow side with purple basil, and the red side with green basil. Serve immediately.

Recommended wine: Baux-de-Provence Rosé 2001, Domaine des Terres-Blanches.

Index
and useful
information

Index of recipes

Warning
There are risks in eating raw fish for people whose immune systems are vulnerable. Raw fish should be avoided by pregnant women, and anyone with reduced immunity, including the elderly and young children.

Dry conversions

Metric	Imperial
10 g	½ oz
20 g	¾ oz
25 g	1 oz
50 g	2 oz
110 g	4 oz
150 g	5 oz
200 g	7 oz
250 g	9 oz
450 g	1 lb
700 g	1⅓ lb
900 g	2 lb

Liquid conversions

Metric	Imperial	US cups
30 ml	1 fl oz	⅛ cup
60 ml	2 fl oz	¼ cup
80 ml	2¾ fl oz	⅓ cup
125 ml	4 fl oz	½ cup
185 ml	6 fl oz	¾ cup
250 ml	8 fl oz	1 cup
375 ml	12 fl oz	1½ cups
500 ml	16 fl oz	2 cups
600 ml	20 fl oz	2½ cups
750 ml	24 fl oz	3 cups
1 litre	32 fl oz	4 cups

Bibliography

Aduriz, A. L., S. Bregaña and A. Edorta. *Bacalao, Ttabula 01, monográficos de cultura y gastronomía.* Barcelona: Montagud Editores, 2003.

Arenós, P. *Los Genios del Fuego.* Barcelona: Península, 1999.

Bacon, J. *Exotic Fruits &Vegetables A–Z.* St. Leonard's, England: UPSO, 2004.

Bataille-Benguigui, M.-C. and F. Cousin, eds. *Cuisines: reflets des sociétés.* Paris: Éditions Sépia—Musée de l'Homme, 1996.

Botella, T. *Cocina para Cóctel.* Barcelona: Montagud Editores, 2003.

Bras, M. *Bras, Laguiole, Aubrac, France.* Rodez, France: Éditions du Rouergue, 2003.

Cedroni, M. *Sushi & Susci.* Lodi, Italy: Biblioteca Culinaria, 2001.

Colicchio, T. *Craft of Cooking.* New York: Clarkson Potter Publishers, 2003.

Custer, T. *The Art of Peruvian Cuisine.* Lima: Ediciones Ganesha, 2000.

Davidson, Alan, ed. *The Oxford Companion to Food.* Oxford: Oxford University Press, 1999.
———. *Mediterranean Seafood.* Second edition. Harmondsworth, UK: Penguin, 1981.
———. *North Atlantic Seafood.* New York: Viking Press, 1980.

Hanbuckers, A. and K. Keygnaert. *Hanbuckers.* Bruges, Belgium: Auberge Herborist, 2002.

Keller, T. *The French Laundry Cookbook.* New York: Artisan, 1999.

Kunz, G. and P. Kaminsky. *The Elements of Taste.* Boston: Little, Brown and Company, 2001.

Lang, Jennifer Harvey, ed. *Larousse Gastronomique.* New American Edition. New York: Crown Publishers, 1995.

Messiaen, C.-M. *Le Potager tropical.* Paris: Éditions Cilf, 1998.
———. *Le Bon Jardinier–Encyclopédie horticole.* Vol. 1. Paris: La Maison rustique.

Nobu, M. *Nobu the Cookbook.* London: Quadrille Publishing House, 2001.

Rodriguez, D. *The Great Ceviche Book.* Berkeley, California: Ten Speed Press, 2003.

Romera, M. S. *La Cocina de los Sentidos.* Barcelona: Planeta, 2003.

Samuelsson, M. *Aquavit and the New Scandinavian Cuisine.* Boston/New York: Houghton Mifflin Company, 2003.

Schneider, E. *Uncommon Fruits &Vegetables.* New York: William Morrow, 1986.
———. *Vegetables, from Amaranth to Zucchini.* New York: William Morrow, 2001.

Sugimoto, T. and M. Iwatate. *Shunju, New Japanese Cuisine.* Singapore: Periplus Editions, 2002.

Teo, M. and D. Bosco *New Chinese Cuisine.* Singapore: Tung Lok Restaurants, 2002.

Tetsuya, W. *Tetsuya.* Berkeley, California: Ten Speed Press, 2001.

Tramonto, R. *Amuse-Bouche: Little Bites of Delight before the Meal Begins.* New York: Random House, 2002.

Troisgros, M. *La Cuisine acidulée de Michel Troisgros.* Paris: Le Cherche Midi, 2002.

Trotter, C. *Charlie Trotter's Seafood.* Berkeley, California: Ten Speed Press, 1997.
———. *The Kitchen Sessions.* Berkeley, California: Ten Speed Press, 1999.

Trotter, C. and R. Klein. *Raw.* Berkeley, California: Ten Speed Press, 2003.

Acknowledgments

To Grant Symon, the eye of the uncooked.

To Françoise and Joël Thiébault for their loyalty and sincerity.

To Armando Manni for his oil and his passion.

To the "guest stars" of *Uncooked*: Iñiaki Aizpitarte for eggs, Laurent Chareau for soy, and Taïra Kurihara for langoustine.

But above all, to all those who in France and throughout the world showed us the way to use raw food: Raquel, Alberto, Jean-François, Gilles, Pascal and Paul in Paris; Olivier in Cancale; Michel and Sébastien in Laguiole; Michel in Roanne; Jacques in Vichy; Jean in Tarare; Heston in Bray; Ferràn in Roses; Moreno in Senigallia; Carlo in Milan; Joan in Gijón; Santi in Sant-Celoni; Hervé in Lima; Charlie in Chicago; Roxane in Larkspur; Nobu in London; Daniel, Douglas, and Jean-Georges in New York; Thomas in Yountville; and Hirohisa in Tokyo.

To the Artyg family and Christophe Auger.

To Béatrice Weité.

To Sylviane Mériel and the Maison Montgolfier.

To Jean-Paul Nadaud and the Maison Bernardaud.

To Magimix.

To the ever-faithful Baptiste Kieken, ever the assistant photographer and ever vigilant.

To Brodie and Sarah for their patience and encouragement.

To Arabella, Marguerite, and Zelda for their good humor and gourmet tastes.

And, last but not least, to Ghislaine Bavoillot, Nathalie Démoulin, and Sylvie Ramaut.

PHOTOGRAPHIC CREDITS
Pages 13, 17, and 19: Patrick Mikanowski; page 22: Reuters; page 24: Bridgeman Art Library.
All other photographs in this book: Grant Symon.

 for the images in this book that were produced on their digital camera backs.

Contact Patrick or Lyndsay Mikanowski at: **contacts@elzear.net**
For more information about ELZEAR: **www.elzear.net**
To learn more about Grant Symon: **www.GrantSymon.com**

RECIPES & ARTISTIC DIRECTION
Patrick Mikanowski

CONCEPT
Elzear@wanadoo.fr

DESIGN
Artyg@wanadoo.fr

TRANSLATED FROM THE FRENCH BY
Josephine Bacon

COPYEDITING
Penelope Isaac

TYPESETTING
Claude-Olivier Four

PROOFREADING
Chrisoula Petridis

Printed in Italy by Errestampa

Distributed in North America by Rizzoli
International Publications, Inc.

Previously published in French as *Cru*
© Éditions Flammarion, 2004
English-language edition
© Éditions Flammarion, 2005

All rights reserved. No part of this
publication may be reproduced in
any form or by any means, electronic,
photocopy, information retrieval system,
or otherwise, without written permission from
Éditions Flammarion.
26, rue Racine
75006 Paris

www.editions.flammarion.com

05 06 07 4 3 2 1

FC0476-05-III
ISBN: 2-0803-0476-3
Dépôt légal: 03/2005